YOUR ROADMAP TO A
CONVERSION-CENTERED
CATECHUMENATE

Your Roadmap to a Conversion-Centered Catechumenate

A Report from the Trenches

John McGlynn

LITURGICAL PRESS

Collegeville, Minnesota

www.litpress.org

1   2   3   4   5   6   7   8   9

Library of Congress Cataloging-in-Publication Data

Names: McGlynn, John, author.
Title: Your roadmap to a conversion-centered catechumenate : a report from the trenches / John McGlynn.
Description: Collegeville, Minnesota : Liturgical Press, [2022] | Summary: "In this 'report from the trenches' the author shows how his parish team was able to transform their process from a traditional academic model to true training in Christian life, focused on the goals of the individual seeker. Through the author's real-world experience readers will discover how to develop their own roadmap to transform and renew their parish initiation processes"— Provided by publisher.
Identifiers: LCCN 2021053764 (print) | LCCN 2021053765 (ebook) | ISBN 9780814667415 (paperback) | ISBN 9780814667422 (epub) | ISBN 9780814667422 (pdf)
Subjects: LCSH: Catechumens. | Initiation rites—Religious aspects—Catholic Church.
Classification: LCC BX935 .M38 2022 (print) | LCC BX935 (ebook) | DDC 265/.13—dc23/eng/20220112
LC record available at https://lccn.loc.gov/2021053764
LC ebook record available at https://lccn.loc.gov/2021053765

To Pat—my best friend, my wife, and my personal theologian

Contents

Acknowledgments

To Sr. Kathleen Morrissey, RSC (RIP), who first brought me and my wife into RCIA ministry.

To Jackie Middaugh, my predecessor and mentor in the RCIA, who introduced me to the North American Forum for the Catechumenate and began our transition to a year-round catechumenate.

To Msgr. Bill O'Keeffe, who as pastor gave me the opportunity and support to continue the evolution of our RCIA process when he appointed me Director of Adult Faith Formation & RCIA.

To the parish community of Our Lady of Refuge, Long Beach, California, whose many dedicated ministers, catechists, staff, and members provide a welcoming environment for all our seekers looking for Christ, for enriching my faith and ministry over the years.

To the parish community of Our Lady of Lourdes, Tujunga, California, and the many people who, after educating me and nurturing me in my youth, introduced me to opportunities in ministry.

To the Archdiocese of Los Angeles Religious Education Congress and the many dedicated organizers, speakers, and supporters of this one-of-a-kind gathering for catechists and ministers, whose many experts, year after year, help me learn and grow in my faith and ministry, providing me with the continual training, knowledge, and spiritual support to spread the Gospel to our seekers.

To my family, Pat, Cecilia, and Genny, for your continual love and support and inspiration.

And most importantly, to Nick Wagner and Diana Macalintal of TeamRCIA, who not only helped me grow in RCIA ministry but also encouraged me to share my experiences through the TeamRCIA blog and with this book. Your friendship and fellowship in Christ are an inspiration and a constant source of renewal.

Introduction

Change can be hard. As human beings we are, by nature, resistant to change. This is particularly true when we think what we currently have now is just fine and doesn't need to change. But there is one undeniable truth: God is not static. We are not static. All creation is alive: growing, changing, evolving! Similarly, our relationship with God isn't static. It's dynamic! We are living, breathing, and constantly evolving—and sometimes that means that we need to alter our course to keep moving in a positive direction.

As catechists we teach, "God always meets us where we're at." But this idea also begs the question: Is our adult initiation process meeting our seekers where *they* are at?

And even if we thought our processes were adequate at the time we implemented them, are they still adequate to where our seekers and our parishes are today?

For many years now, catechumenate leaders have been urging us to examine our processes in ways that can better deliver on the promises of the Rite of Christian Initiation of Adults. We now have a better understanding of the stages of conversion, as embodied in the steps of evangelization and precatechumenate, catechumenate, purification and enlightenment, and mystagogy, as well as a recognition that someone's desire to begin the process may not always follow a traditional academic calendar. This is why moving to an ongoing year-round process is so important.

Imagine for a moment a person who has been thinking about becoming Catholic and, after weeks or months (or even years) of consideration, finds the courage to call the parish office, only to be told that the process has already started and that they should call back again in the fall. I'm sure many of you are familiar with this scenario because I've seen it play out far too many times, including at my own parish.

Is this how we invite people into relationship with Christ? I'm sure you will agree that the answer to this question should be a resounding no! But how exactly do we foster our catechumens' relationship with Christ? How can we move from a traditional academic model to an ongoing year-round process? What does it really take in terms of actions, time, and resources?

It's Not as Hard as You Might Think

Having moved to a year-round process in my own parish, I've been able to identify a series of steps that you can use to move your process to an ongoing year-round apprenticeship model. This kind of change doesn't happen overnight, but I'm confident that by learning from my experience, you too can bring your parish initiation processes into an effective year-round model. I also think you will find it will have a number of benefits:

- Making the process more welcoming for seekers

- Making the management of your process much easier, particularly with limited resources

- Making your catechetical sessions more relevant and dynamic

- Making better disciples

I realize that change is difficult, especially when it comes to your parish initiation processes. You immediately start thinking about all the reasons why this or that can't be done or what additional resources might be needed. But I ask you to prayerfully consider this: Change is our business. The people who come to us are looking for change and they're coming to us to find it. The change they're looking for is bringing God into (or back into) their lives, and they are looking to our Catholic faith as that path. The whole catechumenate process (as well as all sacramental preparation) is one of changing our lives to be more like Christ. Change like that takes time, patience, prayer, and fortitude, all of which we as catechists and team members try to provide through our initiation processes.

So if you think changing your process is something that can't be done, I challenge you to think again. Just as with our seekers, it won't be accomplished overnight, but I like to think if my own parish can do it, so can yours.

Chapter 1

How to Begin

If you're a fan of superhero films, you're familiar with the concept of an "origin story." These are the background stories of our protagonists (and their antagonists) that tell us how they came to be the people they are today.

Origin stories serve an important purpose in our human culture, as well. They ground us in a common mythos of our past in order to help us understand the present and where we want to go as a people or society in the future. Origin stories tell of great successes as well as failures in order to form a society's understanding of its beginning, its purpose, and its mission.

As church we also have an origin story—the book of Genesis. Here, we are introduced to our Lord God and how through his love he created us and our universe. As with any good origin story, ours is important in helping us to understand God and God's love for us. And don't think for a moment that the ancient scribes who compiled this text didn't have this very idea in mind when they put quill to parchment. Without an origin story, we wouldn't understand that God made us out of love, which would make everything that comes after Genesis much more confusing.

I love a good origin story. I think it's one of the reasons I became attracted to adult initiation ministry. All seekers have an origin story—how it is that they came knocking on our parish door. And while many stories can be similar, none of them are exactly the same. Seekers' origin stories are as unique as they are, and I find each one fascinating.

Not only that, but their perspectives tend to be very different from mine. I was raised Catholic. My four siblings and I attended Catholic school through high school, just as our parents did. I like to joke that because of my family's Irish and Italian ancestry from Brooklyn I didn't have a choice but to be Catholic. Of course, there comes a point in our lives when we "cradle Catholics" do need to make a commitment to the church, but that's a story for another time. Suffice it to say, growing up Catholic wasn't something we chose—it was something we were.

I think that's why I'm so fascinated with our adult seekers. They are making a choice. They are choosing to become one of us! As rational, thinking adults, they are choosing to follow Christ in the Catholic tradition, with all the church's graces and flaws. I think that takes a lot of courage—a courage I wonder if I could muster had I been raised in different circumstances.

In a way, adult initiation is all about origin stories, since we help seekers to find out where they've been and where they are now, in order to help them chart a path toward Christ.

Why Are You Here? What's Your Origin Story?

Origin stories are part of our business, so as a matter of practice, I think it's important for all of us in this ministry to remember our own origin stories. Not only does it help us maintain a certain perspective when talking with seekers, it can remind us of why we're in this ministry.

When taking on a ministry, whether you are new to that ministry or have been involved for some time, I think it's important to periodically remind yourself of your own origin story and consider why you are here doing it. What lead you to this point? Why are you here now? Whether you've been a longtime catechist or this is your first time as a catechist, you should take a moment to consider your origin story about why you're involved in catechumenate ministry.

Why is this exercise important? It helps to build agency. It helps to create ownership. Just as with our church's origin story, it reminds us of why we are here. So before you go on a mission to renew your parish initiation process, I think the first important step is to remember why you are here and why you're doing this. Renewing your parish initiation process takes a commitment, a vow to lead people to Christ. Are you up to the challenge?

"No Experience Required"

If you're like me, this is what you were told when you were asked to join the initiation team. When I started, I knew almost nothing about the catechumenate process. I had some experience as a catechist and some understanding of the rites, but I knew nothing of the actual catechetical or preparation process. Even though I had some training and experience, I still felt completely lost.

Almost no one goes into this ministry as an expert, and almost no one goes into it without being asked. In fact, that's the nature of most any parish ministry—we get thrown in and learn as we go. So don't for a minute think that I started out as an expert in adult initiation. Still, I like to think I'm in good company, because even the apostles themselves were not experts when they started following Jesus. They relied on each other—their community—to help them through. And they had a good teacher in Jesus, who is also our best teacher.

Over the years I've learned a lot from some of the best, some from my own parish and many more from outside my parish. I was an active participant in moving our parish initiation process from a one-size-fits-all academic exercise to an ongoing year-round apprenticeship model that respects each seeker's experience and needs. And as the old saying goes, if we can do it, so can you.

Also, as members of the church, the Body of Christ, we learn that we are more than just followers of Christ: we are stewards of the faith. And that faith is a gift, given by Christ, first to his apostles and his disciples and, eventually, through the millennia, to us. And this gift, once given, needs to be shared. So if my experience in adult formation and initiation can be of benefit to anyone else, then I am duty-bound by my baptism to share it for the benefit of all of us.

Also, please keep in mind that just as there's no such thing as a one-size-fits-all catechumenate process (which you will learn more about as you continue reading), there's no one single approach or "silver bullet" to making your parish process the best it can be. Every community is different, and each has their unique challenges. So while this book is meant to be a roadmap to successfully transform your initiation processes, it is also meant to be adapted to your parish's situation and needs. Look at it as a guide for best practices learned from someone who has lived in the trenches of parish initiation ministry. I think there's a lot here that can help you, and in the process, maybe you will learn something that you can share with someone else.

It Starts with Team Formation

There's a difference between "training" and "formation," just as there's a difference between calling ourselves "catechists" as opposed to "teachers." Yes, as catechists we often make use of those tools found in a teacher's toolbox, just as training is one of the tools we use in formation. For some people, this is all just semantics, but I disagree. Words matter. The language we use matters. Forming a team is much more than training a team. Forming an initiation team means getting everyone on the same page—not just with best practices but with a good understanding of themselves and their gifts so the talents of the entire team can be leveraged for the greater good.

The first part of team formation should look very similar to how we approach a typical seeker. This is something a parish team can do on their own, but it can help by having someone outside the team facilitate this exercise. You want to ask the team these questions about your parish initiation process:

- Where have you been?

- Where are you now?

Put another way, what is your parish's initiation origin story? Think about it—a seeker who comes to us is looking to renew something in their life. Maybe it's a call to form a relationship with God. Maybe it's a call to renew or reconnect with one's faith. Or maybe it's a call to continue one's faith journey through the Catholic tradition. Regardless, our seekers are looking for something that's missing in their lives. These same questions can be and should be applied to a parish's initiation process when you're seeking to renew that process. What has your parish done well? What didn't go so well? Understanding where you've been and where you are now gives you a good starting point from which to begin your renewal.

When our parish first started its renewal process, our director took us on a one-day retreat. We went to one of the local retreat houses and addressed these two questions as a team.

Now, I can hear some of you scoffing at the idea of going to a retreat house. "We don't have the money for that!" Neither did we. It just so happened that our director had a good friend who was a religious sister, and she let us use one of their common rooms for the day. So if your parish is like mine, where resources can be limited, it can be helpful to reach out to others or to call in a few favors so your team can meet outside of the parish facilities. There is some benefit from being away from the "familiar," especially when your goal is to turn your process away from the familiar.

Of course, if you can't take your team "off campus," you can still try to bring that "away from home" feeling by meeting in a space where you don't normally meet. It could be at a team member's home, or it could be in the parish teacher's lounge or the rectory garden—someplace other than your normal meeting room or parish hall. And if at all possible, stay away from school class-rooms (more on that later).

Also, when you meet to discuss these questions, make sure someone is taking notes. Assign someone to be the scribe to document the discussion, and have that person share their notes with the entire team. You will want these notes on hand when you begin the next phase of your renewal discussion.

Reviewing these questions in a retreat-type setting not only allows team members to share in the discussion, but it also works as a team-building exercise. Remember when I mentioned reviewing your own origin story? This could be a good icebreaker activity at the beginning of the session. Exploring everyone's personal origin stories can be a good catalyst for breaking into a discussion on the parish's initiation origin story.

Training Is Key

Once you as a team have reviewed where you've been and where you are now, the next step is question number three:

- Where do you want to get to?

This is perhaps the hardest question because how do you know where you want to go if you've never been there? If you've never seen it?

Let's look at this from another angle: How do you know what your initiation process can be if you haven't seen what it could be?

This is where some form of outside or third-party training is vital. Here you need to reach outside the bubble of your parish to something bigger. Of course, this is one of the joys of being part of the larger universal church—there are plenty of resources beyond our parish which we can take advantage of.

Now, I realize that in many parishes, one-on-one style training is the norm, especially in those that have limited resources or where timing doesn't allow someone to get outside training before they can start on the team. This usually means that a new catechist is paired with an experienced catechist so that the new person can learn from the veteran. This is a valuable tool, but it should not be your only tool.

Training is an essential part of every profession. Not only do many professions require a certificate or college degree, but many professions and trades have tests and are monitored by state boards. Further, many of these professions require ongoing training or the earning of CEUs (continuing education units) in order to maintain their credentials. Why all this training and testing and monitoring? It's to protect us—the people whom these professionals serve—to make sure everyone who engages their services is getting the best possible care, attention, or service.

The church, in her wisdom, requires the same for all of us engaged in catechetical ministry. Every diocese has some kind of process for the formation and training of catechists. Unfortunately, for those of us working as initiation coordinators and ministers, basic catechist formation is not enough. The special conditions of addressing adult needs and the considerations laid out in the rite require that we seek additional training specific to our ministry. It's the only way in which you can begin to see what your initiation process could be. And like the other professionals I mention above, this training isn't so much for us: it's for those whom we serve.

In addition to the many years I've spent as a catechist, I've also spent most of my life as a volunteer leader in scouting. There we have a phrase: "Every scout deserves a trained leader." When I think of my daughter working her way up the trail to Eagle Scout, I most certainly want to make sure that her troop leaders are trained and experienced. Only those who are well trained can guide her effectively to her goals. Knowing this, it isn't a stretch to consider that this same ideal applies to initiation ministry. To paraphrase, "Every seeker deserves a trained catechist."

What does formal training provide that makes it so important?

- It builds community.

  There's no substitution for the grace we receive celebrating as a community of believers. Jesus taught us this as he gathered his apostles and disciples. In community we find strength and unity of purpose. It shows us that we're not alone and that we can learn from each other as we share similar challenges and build relationships with our fellow initiation ministers.

- It forms a unified vision.

  The goal of leading adults to full initiation in the church may be our common goal, but we also need to make sure we're all on the same page with how best to lead them there. I will never forget the utter confusion I had when I first read the Rite of Christian Initiation of Adults. Only through training did I come to understand its intent and meaning and how we could translate those requirements to a process that met the needs of our parish community.

- It makes us better catechists.

  Training isn't meant to show us what we're doing wrong; it's meant to show us how we can be better. As proud as I am with what we've been able to accomplish at my parish, I'm also well aware of those areas where we still need to improve. No process is beyond the need to improve. Jesus himself always pushed his disciples to do more (Mark 10:17-25), to go one step further. We should do the same.

- It gives you and your team confidence.

  Whenever I'm recruiting new team members, the most common sentiment I hear (second only to "I don't have the time") is, "I don't know what I'm doing." But here's the truth: We've all been there. No one who starts in this ministry started as an expert. I certainly wasn't. I became the initiation director

I am today only after having a lot of training and working with other more experienced leaders.

- It can be the catalyst to move your process forward.

  I've met many initiation catechists who recognized the need for change but didn't know where to start. No process is going to change overnight, nor should it. Only through training can you and your team gain the knowledge and skills needed to identify what needs to change and how to prioritize those changes in a way that is best for your community.

Know When to Hold 'Em.
Know When to Fold 'Em.

If there's anything I've learned from a lifetime in Catholic schools, it's learning how to make do with what you have and then making it better—turning what seems to be a losing hand into a winning hand.

We Catholics have a history of being the scrappy underdogs, working with limited resources and a can-do spirit to make things happen. That same scrappy insurgent spirit still lives on in our local parishes, especially where resources are scarce and needs are great. It's how we manage to survive and thrive, and it helps to bind us into a community.

Unfortunately, there's also a dark side to this parish can-do spirit—parishioners and parish leaders can begin to think that they don't need anyone else's help.

One of the joys of being part of the universal church is the many resources available to us, many of which are free or for minimal cost. Among them are:

- Your own pastor and others in your parish leadership team, including associate pastors, deacons, pastoral associates, directors of formation, and even the school principal. In many parishes, the catechumenate team lives in its own bubble within the parish, sticking its head out only during Lent. By reaching out to other parish individuals and groups, you might be pleasantly surprised. You never know where you might find a helpful resource (or even some new seekers). Not only can your initiation process benefit from these other parish groups, but it can help integrate your initiation process into the wider parish community.

- Other local parishes. Make an effort to reach out and get to know the people working in catechumenate ministry and adult faith formation in your neighboring parishes. Find out what they're doing and who else they know. In business organizations we are constantly taught the value of networking to help build our careers. The same is true for ministry. So make the effort to reach out and get to know more people working in this ministry in your local area.

- Diocesan resources. Many dioceses have personnel dedicated to helping initiation catechists. Don't know where to start? How about your diocesan web site? Or contact the person who coordinates the Rite of Election. Many dioceses also hold or sponsor workshops and conferences that can be helpful to initiation catechists, or they may hold regular group meetings of initiation or formation directors. Make contacts and get on their email lists.

- TeamRCIA: Founded as an internet community to connect and support initiation ministers, TeamRCIA.com is a free resource for Catholic parishes and dioceses that want to form Christians for life. They offer a free weekly newsletter and free webinars, as well as a paid subscription with a number of additional resources. Additionally, TeamRCIA offers a number of live training sessions throughout the year. Take a moment and go to their website to see where and when they might be hosting a live workshop someplace near you.

- Feeling adventurous? Why not go out of town to attend an even bigger conference? Many larger dioceses or book publishers will sponsor major workshops and events that support initiation teams. A quick internet search can find any number of conferences and training opportunities.

While there may be talented and experienced individuals within your parish community, my experience over the years has been that the best formation comes from reaching outside the comfortable bubble of your own parish. Consider for a moment all our seekers, some of whom have never had any religious formation or identity. Now imagine how far outside their comfort zone they've had to reach in order to make their initial inquiries. We can learn a lot from their courage to seek a change in their lives.

Team training allows you to see both what is possible and proper for preparing the rites and for crafting your own initiation processes—and not just once. Team training and formation should remain regular and ongoing.

As initiation catechists, we remind our catechumens and candidates that their baptism (or reception into full communion) isn't an end, but a beginning. In fact, we spend the entire period of mystagogy helping them to process the experience of their initiation and to help them chart the course on the next step of their faith journey. We as catechists must practice what we preach. One moment of formal formation is just the first step in what should be a continuing journey of formation.

Like Jesus going to the wilderness, we too must get away—to refresh ourselves, to pray, and to discern how we can continually make our rites and processes better. Training and formation helps us draw the map that gets us there.

Paragraph 4 of the rite states, "The initiation of catechumens is a gradual process that takes place in the community of the faithful." The same can be said for moving your initiation process to an ongoing year-round model. We need to reach beyond ourselves to the parish community and the greater Catholic community for support and guidance. Even Jesus knew he could not accomplish his mission alone—and neither should we.

Chapter 2

Throw Out Your Syllabus

After team formation, the next step to moving to an ongoing year-round process is simple: Throw out your syllabus.

Hear me out on this one: Have you noticed there's not much out there when it comes to an "off-the-shelf" program for the catechumenate? There's a reason for that, but more on that in a moment. This lack of a defined program has left most of us to develop our own programs (which isn't necessarily a bad thing).

As a result, many initiation teams and leaders (myself included) would gather together and lovingly craft a "course of study" that they feel every good Catholic should know. We crafted it so that all the "important" topics can be covered over the course of the school year (typically seven or eight months).

The reality, however, is that regardless of whatever we've crafted in the past (with all the best of intentions), one curriculum just is not and will never be sufficient. What I've explained to seekers over the years also applies here to initiation catechists: The catechumenate is not a series of "classes" you take in order to "graduate" as a Catholic. Rather, it is a process of conversion to the Christian life.

Put another way, the catechumenate is not just about learning the faith; it's about living the faith. And to help our catechumens and candidates do this, we need to put aside the traditional academic model in favor of a model that weaves the seekers into the fabric of parish life.

The RCIA Is Not an Academic Process, It's an Apprenticeship

Perhaps the hardest part of throwing out our syllabuses is changing our own perspectives. When I started in initiation ministry many years ago, we ran with a traditional academic model, like most parishes at the time. We began our process in September, aligning with the school calendar. We gathered people into a single group or "cohort" and followed a lecture-style presentation based on our carefully crafted syllabus. Everything about our process fell in line with traditional academics. And why not? It seems to work well for children's religious education. And what is the catechumenate but religious education for adults, right?

Wrong!

While an academic model may be effective for teaching, it's not very effective for forming people to live the faith—not for children and certainly not for adults. It's not the way we bring people into a relationship with Christ. Jesus didn't use a syllabus, so why should we? We're in the business of evangelizing! The *Directory for Catechesis* states:

> Evangelizing is not, in the first place, the delivery of a doctrine; but rather, making present and announcing Jesus Christ. (29)

Now, to be fair, we don't want to throw out everything from our academic toolbox. After all, much of our catechetical training has its origin and practices in the world of education, and many of our catechists come from academic backgrounds. But we also need to remember that when it comes to forming adults in the faith, we need to make a conscious effort to move past the academic format.

We also need to consider that adults who are not in school or don't have school age kids don't follow the academic calendar. Discarding the academic calendar includes embracing a language and a process that allows us to bring individuals to Christ, not teach classes to students. Remember, the catechumenate is not about learning the faith; it's about living the faith.

Watch Your Language

Perhaps one of the most effective ways of changing our perspective is changing the language we use about the process. This can be a challenge—not only because we've become so accustomed to using academic language when working in formation ministry but our audience, our seekers, as well as most everyone else in the parish, also use academic language when referring to formation or sacrament preparation.

"When do your classes start?" If you're a catechumenate coordinator, you probably hear this question on a regular basis. Most times you hear it from seekers, but I've also heard it from our own parish staff.

I have two problems with this question. First is the use of the word "classes." Second is with the word "start." The word "classes" assumes that the faith is something that can be taught. It can't. And the word "start" assumes a common point of entry, which there is not.

For too many years, the catechumenate—and all catechetical formation—has been steeped in academic language. It made sense at the time, especially when you consider that catechetical formation was an extension of what our Catholic schools were providing, often by those same priests, sisters, and brothers who ran our parochial schools. But now, in the twenty-first century, we've come to realize that this use of academic language has clouded our perception of what it takes to become a Catholic. Our faith is much more than an academic exercise. It is a way of life. Our faith is not a series of abstract notions of a creator but rather a relationship with the living Christ and his church.

So in order to better clarify what we do as initiation catechists, we need to be conscious and deliberate in our use of catechetical language for everything we do.

We should never use the word "teacher" or "instructor." Instead, we should employ "catechist" or "facilitator."

We should never use the word "class" when referring to our catechetical sessions. Instead, use the word "session" or "meeting" or "gathering." And related to that, never refer to the collective group as a "class." The word "class" infers that everyone is on a common path with a defined beginning and conclusion. Instead, use the word "group," which has a certain flexibility that allows each individual to be on their own path even though we may gather together for shared catechetical sessions.

We should never refer to our seekers as "students." This is an academic term that doesn't fully encompass a catechumen's or candidate's position within the church. Yes, as a catechumen, seekers officially become "learners" within the church, but I would argue there's a difference between being a "student" and being a "learner." The word student evokes an academic endeavor, whereas the word learner evokes something more personal. A student "studies" their topic—there's an inherent detachment in the endeavor. A learner, on the other hand, is "apprenticed" to a "vocation." *Ad Gentes* (Decree on the Church's Missionary Activity) reminds us:

> [The catechumenate] is not merely an exposition of dogmatic truths and norms of morality, but a period of formation in the entire Christian life, an apprenticeship of suitable duration, during which the disciples will be joined to Christ their Teacher. (14)

The process of the catechumenate is an apprenticeship in which learners, and we, are learning to live the faith. Becoming a Catholic is a lifelong vocation, not just a course of study.

And when it comes to our scheduling of sessions, we should avoid using the words "start" or "finish" as they relate to our calendar. There is no beginning or end in an ongoing, year-round process. Even when we're not holding formal catechetical sessions, catechetical formation still continues within the parish community and every week by participating in Sunday Mass.

Now, some would argue that all this concern about using precise terms in the catechumenate is unnecessary. But I disagree. The words and the language we use both create and reflect our understanding, so we need to be conscious of the words we're using and change our habits accordingly. And not only that, we need to catechize our fellow catechists, parish staff, and parish leaders on the importance of using the right language, especially when addressing seekers.

Let us never forget that words are serious business in our faith tradition. When God uses a word, it comes into being.

- Genesis 1:3: "Then God said: Let there be light, and there was light."

- Isaiah 55:11: "So shall my word be that goes forth from my mouth; It shall not return to me empty, but shall do what pleases me, achieving the end for which I sent it."

- John 1:1: "In the beginning was the Word, and the Word was with God, and the Word was God."

- John 1:14a "And the Word became flesh and made his dwelling among us."

Words have power. Words shape our perceptions. As catechists, our words and our actions are the tools we use to evangelize and spread the Gospel. So it stands to reason that we should be very careful with the words we use when engaging in catechesis and evangelization. So the next time someone asks, "When do your classes start?" my answer is, "The process begins right now."

Take Formation Out of the Classroom

We also need to look at where we're having our catechetical sessions. If at all possible, we should avoid using a classroom. Classrooms only reinforce the idea of initiation being an academic process instead of a personal journey of faith. Not only that, the very layout of the space, with desks, white boards, and audio-visual equipment, only reinforces a power structure (teacher above students) over that of a shared discussion among equals (seekers and facilitator).

If you have no other choice—and I do recognize that in some parishes finding an alternative can be difficult—at least bring the desks into a circle so everyone can face each other. It would be much better if you could find a conference room, meeting room, lounge, or other comfortable space—a more "adult" space. Even a school cafeteria would be preferable to a classroom. Taking sessions out of a classroom reinforces the idea that, rather than attending a class, participants are gathering for an interactive experience. This works best when everyone in the group can see everyone else, like sitting in a circle or around a conference table. If you have a particularly large group, you may need to set up several tables in a larger space.

And regardless of where you meet, you should also give some attention to the décor of the space. Consider the liturgical colors and elements of the season and items related to the week's topic (e.g., bowl of water for baptism, or an Advent wreath for Advent). Use tablecloths, centerpieces, banners, and other elements that evoke the themes of the season. If you don't have any skills in this area, talk with someone in your parish who does. And since the space is likely shared by others, come up with something that can be taken out and put away easily. It doesn't need to be elaborate, but it should be deliberate, and it should help bring your church's seasonal environment into your meeting space. Candles (if allowed) also make for a nice focal point during prayer.

Moving Beyond Your Syllabus

So if you throw out the syllabus, what do you do? As I noted earlier, there isn't much available as far as an "out-of-the-box" catechumenate process. That's because there's no "one-size-fits-all" model that can be developed for a journey of faith and conversion.

There are just too many variables, both among the catechumens and candidates and within each parish community. There are, however, a wealth of tools and experience available that can help us re-craft a process that effectively brings our seekers into the active life of the church.

Let the Liturgy Be Your Guide

Our job as initiation catechists is to bring our seekers into the active life of the parish, which centers on Sunday Mass. As Catholics, participating in Sunday Mass is the most visible and consistent expression of our faith, so it stands to reason that those looking to join us should follow that same rubric. This is why the rite says:

> From the very beginning of the period of the catechumenate the catechumens should be taught to keep holy the Lord's Day. (83)

Chances are, it was attending a Mass that got many of your seekers interested in the Catholic faith. Attending Mass not only allows them the opportunity to engage with the parish community, but it also serves as a living, learning environment for the Christian life. Letting the Sunday Mass serve as your guide not only keeps with the spirit of the rite, paragraphs 81–89, but when taken as a whole, reflects what the Constitution on the Sacred Liturgy states:

> In the course of the year, moreover, it [the church] unfolds the whole mystery of Christ from the incarnation and nativity to the ascension, to Pentecost and the expectation of the blessed hope of the coming of the Lord.
>
> Thus recalling the mysteries of the redemption, [the church] opens up to the faithful the riches of the Lord's powers and merits, so that these are in some way made present at all times; the faithful lay hold of them and are filled with saving grace. (102)

This point alone would seem to necessitate an ongoing catechumenate that has our seekers participating in that process for an extended period. The U.S. National Statutes for the Catechumenate state that the period of the catechumenate should "extend for at least one year" (6). That's a far more modest understanding than RCIA 7.2, which states that the period of the catechumenate "may last for several years."

Perhaps the most important takeaway is this: We're not on a fixed timetable. Through the initiation process, we are looking to "play the long game" by allowing Christ to reveal himself through our people and our stories—not only those stories we share through the Scriptures but those we share as being part of the parish community in our lived experience of Christ. Pope Francis stated in his apostolic exhortation *Evangelii Gaudium*:

> Pastoral ministry in a missionary style is not obsessed with the disjointed transmission of a multitude of doctrines to be insistently imposed. When we adopt a pastoral goal and a missionary style which would actually reach everyone without exception or exclusion, the message has to concentrate on the essentials, on what is most beautiful, most grand, most appealing and at the same time most necessary. The message is simplified, while losing none of its depth and truth, and thus becomes all the more forceful and convincing. (35)

Using the Liturgy and the Rites as Your Guide for Catechesis

The *Rite of Christian Initiation of Adults* is an elegant document designed to show us that initiation into the faith isn't an academic exercise but rather a series of "steps marking the catechumens' progress" (6). Preparing for these steps isn't done in a classroom following a syllabus; it is best accomplished through the enthusiastic engagement of the catechumens in the life of the parish community—through their active participation in the Sunday liturgy and their progress through the rites celebrated in the midst of the community. This is all another way of saying that any catechetical sessions we have need to be subordinate to the liturgy and truths revealed in the liturgical cycle.

So instead of having your catechetical sessions focus on elements of church teaching and doctrine, they should focus on the lived experience of the participants—what they hear during Mass, what they experience from the rites, how they see Christ through their interactions with the community. The biggest problem with an initiation process that follows a syllabus is that the subject matter is disconnected from the lived experience of the seeker. By using the liturgical calendar as a guide, learners can focus on what they are experiencing in the parish and at Mass, thus enabling them to draw connections between what the church teaches and what they experience.

The Importance of Using the Scriptures in Your Process

During the Rite of Acceptance, seekers accept the way of the Gospel and hear the Gospel proclaimed for the first time as catechumens. Many sponsors will present their catechumens with the gift of a Bible after the liturgy. This is both symbolic and practical. Symbolically, it recognizes the catechumens' desire to follow the way of Christ. By presenting them with a Bible, we are giving them the gateway to Christ, with the practical intention that they should actually read it. But the Bible is no ordinary book. We need to help them learn how to read it—to give them the key to opening that gateway to the Scriptures. One key that can open the Scriptures is our Sunday Mass readings.

You might be saying this all sounds nice in theory, but there's no way this will work in my parish. I get that. I was one of those people saying "It can't work" years ago at my own parish. I'm not just sharing theories here. The point of this book is to share with you how we did it—how we moved to an ongoing process and how letting the Lectionary become our guide actually facilitated that process.

What Does Throwing Out Your Syllabus Look Like?

Just because you're throwing out your syllabus doesn't mean eliminating your catechetical sessions. You still need to prepare some kind of schedule that works for your seekers and your community. So what, then, is the difference between a syllabus and a schedule?

A syllabus reflects a course of study—certain topics presented in a certain order in a way that accomplishes the goals of the class in an orderly manner and within a specified time frame. A schedule, on the other hand, isn't ruled by topics or a course of study. It is ruled by the seasons and the availability of your seekers, with the understanding that to gather together periodically for some mystagogical catechesis is a benefit to the overall process. This allows them to share and discover Christ moving in their daily lives, as well as to consider how the church's teachings are revealed by their lived experience—through their lives, through their interaction with the community, and through what they learn participating in Sunday Mass. Such a schedule should take into consideration both the needs of your seekers and your community.

Don't Plan Your Schedule in a Bubble

A big part of becoming Catholic is becoming part of a community, so we need to give due consideration to what's going on in our community so we can work with and within that community. To borrow from *Gaudium et Spes*, the Pastoral Constitution on the Church in the Modern World from the Second Vatican Council, "[We must now] consider the presence of the church in the world, and its life and activity there" (40).

In other words, we as leaders of the catechumenate need to recognize that we exist in the context of our world, including within our parish community.

When our team plans our schedule, I make sure to have the following items in front of us:

- The liturgical calendar

- The Sunday Lectionary

- The parish calendar

- The diocesan calendar with holy days of obligation, special feast days, and other important events (like the Rite of Election)

- The school calendar (since our parish has a school, and their events impact the parish)

- The religious education calendar (since we share facilities and resources)

- Other community calendars (like local colleges and universities) that may impact your group

Plan Your Schedule for the Full Calendar Year

As we have discussed, the RCIA cannot be fully implemented on a September-to-May calendar. Instead, plan at least a full calendar year in advance, from Advent to Advent or Pentecost to Pentecost. Typically, I will go even further than that. Our parish starts its planning for the next year around Pentecost, and we extend that calendar all the way to December of the following year (at the rollover of the new liturgical year). That way, when we begin our scheduling for the next cycle, we've already got a good head start.

Try to Align Certain Catechetical Topics with the Liturgical Season

The themes of the seasons and the Sunday readings make for a good jumping-off point for discussion on important Catholic teachings. A session on baptism works very well when we celebrate the Baptism of the Lord. A session on the sacrament of reconciliation or prayer works well at almost any time during Lent or Advent. There are any number of resources that can be used to help you find the themes for the seasons and the Sundays and feasts during those seasons. When your session topics align with the liturgical seasons, your seekers can begin to see how these smaller moments flow into the larger rhythm of parish life and of the church. The best learning happens when seekers can see a connection between what's happening in the greater church community and the topics of lived catechesis.

Incorporate the Sunday Liturgy into Your Process

When I say you need to be incorporating Sunday Mass into your process, I'm not suggesting that you should organize your process so that everyone attends the same Sunday Mass. I know a lot of parishes do this, but it wasn't something that worked in my parish. Plus, I like to give our seekers the same flexibility all Catholics have to attend whatever Mass best fits their schedule.

Bringing the experience of Sunday Mass into your catechetical sessions can be accomplished two ways:

- Reflecting back on the previous Sunday's liturgy

- Preparing for the coming Sunday's liturgy

In a mystagogical approach, it is a matter of practice to look back on previous events to see where we have encountered Christ. That can include looking back on the previous Sunday's Mass. An invitation to comment on what catechumens heard or experienced at Mass becomes a jumping-off point for group discussion.

Next, spending some time with the readings for the upcoming Sunday's Mass can help the group see the continuity and continuation of the story that the season is presenting. It also provides the opportunity for discussion and questions that might reveal themselves while going through those readings. Here, the facilitator guides the discussion toward a deeper understanding of the context of the readings, as well as the church's teachings and traditions related to those readings. This can serve as a springboard to a more mystagogical discussion about what the catechumens heard and felt, allowing the facilitator to show how those feelings and insights reveal Christ working in their lives, even when they may not realize it.

There are some added benefits to this approach. Not only does it make the Mass more relevant to your seekers, but for catechists, there's no longer a need to plan out specific topics of discussion.

Instead, you let the topics and themes of the readings serve as the basis of your discussion. Our job isn't to teach on these topics so much as it is to facilitate a discussion on how we can see Christ and the church's teachings through these readings.

In my parish, after we've opened our session with prayer and had a chance to reflect on the previous week's events, we take some time to prepare for the coming Sunday's liturgy. We have our seekers volunteer to proclaim the readings (because I find that helps them get comfortable with the Scriptures), and after each reading, we reflect on what we all heard. Here also, our discussion facilitators take the opportunity to bring some context to the readings, such as how they connect with each other. We also touch on who the authors were and who their original audiences were in order to see how the passages fit into the liturgical season as well as the larger story of salvation history.

I have found that by giving them this opportunity to prepare, they can enter the liturgy more comfortably and eagerly because they're already familiar with the readings. The benefit I've seen is that this practice draws them deeper into the Word, the homily, and the entire liturgy. I have also found this to be effective no matter where people may be on their faith journeys, so seekers don't experience any sense of having "missed" a session that following a syllabus might cause. And for those who have been in the process for a while and heard these readings before, it's an opportunity to experience them anew based on where they are in their journey now.

Changing the Pace

By letting the seasons guide our formation, we need to understand that the overall pace of the process is going to change. In an ongoing, year-round approach, we're moving away from a teaching model where we're trying to cram everything into a fixed timetable to a more relaxed pace where the rhythm of the seasons provide the guide for our catechetical formation. Instead of preparing lessons, we're sharing stories. The focus for our catechumens is not so much what they need to prepare for the next session but what they can expect and experience as the narrative of the seasons unfolds. This slower liturgical pace allows our seekers to enter more fully into the life of the church (and the rest of the parish), and through that, we allow Christ to reveal himself to them in due course—not according to our schedule, but his.

Piggyback Your Needs with What's Already Going On in the Parish

Whenever and wherever possible, don't reinvent the wheel. Instead, make use of the resources already available in your parish. For example, one of our associate pastors is always reminding me about how those in the catechumenate should engage in some form of social outreach. "Great," you say, "but I just don't have the time to plan something like that." But here's the thing, you don't have to, nor should you, do this—on your own. I haven't seen a parish yet that doesn't have someone or some group that already engages in social outreach. Get to know them and see how you can work together. Make use of all the various activities your parish is already doing and have your seekers engage with them.

Facing the Challenge of Summer

Perhaps the hardest part of developing an ongoing process is the fact that many parishes tend to go into "shut-down" mode during the summer. Does an ongoing process mean having regular catechetical sessions throughout the summer? Not necessarily. In fact, there's nothing in the rite that talks about weekly catechetical sessions. How you engage in formal sessions and how often is up to the needs of your seekers and the community during the summer, as well as the rest of the year.

If you look hard enough, there's always something going on at the parish, even during the summer. If there's not much, you might try hosting some of your own community-building activities, such as activities where your initiation ministry can reach out to the rest of the community for some special event. This doesn't need to be elaborate. Examples include field trips to your cathedral or other historic churches and sites. You can plan a summer picnic, host a video night or a video/discussion series, or offer a short retreat or day of prayer. There's any number of different activities that can be planned during the summer months, none of which you and your team necessarily need to plan entirely yourselves. Your own seekers are also a resource that can be tapped, as are other parish groups. All this is in addition to the most important activity that continues to happen in almost every parish even in summer. That's the Sunday Mass.

The main point is that in an ongoing process, you never go completely dark. You continue to maintain contact with everyone continuing on with the process. You continue to be engaged in the activities of the parish. And most importantly, you are always prepared to welcome new seekers and find ways to introduce them to the parish community, even when you may be taking a break from regular catechetical sessions.

I like to remind all my fellow catechists, as well as all our parish staff (especially those who may be taking phone calls from or talking with seekers): If the Holy Spirit is calling someone to our door, who are we to say, "Come back later"? We need to be prepared to receive them like Christ, with open arms.

Be Open and Be Flexible

One of my favorite rites in the initiation process is the Ephphetha Rite. Here, right before the Easter Vigil, we pray with the elect to "be opened" to the Holy Spirit as they prepare for the sacraments of initiation. It's also a good lesson for us as initiation catechists to be open to embracing changes to our processes. On a more practical note, it helps to be flexible as you develop and fine-tune your process. Some things will work and some things won't—or maybe not right away. You will need to implement, evaluate, and move on. This works not only for transforming your process, but it is something you should continue to do on a regular basis.

Have Faith

I've talked with a number of initiation catechists who feel that this approach is radical and unworkable . . . some pie-in-the-sky ideas that can't possibly work. But what we suggest here is neither radical nor unworkable. It's just different from what many of you may have experienced. Many parishes, including my own, have successfully implemented an ongoing, liturgically based process, so we know it can work. A little faith in the Holy Spirit can take you a long way.

Chapter 3

Turning the Initiation Process into an Individual Journey

I've spent quite a few pages here walking you through how to move to an ongoing, year-round process, much of which takes some preparation and planning. I know some of you are eager to get started right away. I'm often asked, "What's one thing we can do right now that can help move us to an ongoing process—something where we don't have to scrap everything we already have in place?" My answer is this: Stop seeing your seekers as a group and see them as the individuals they are.

This book can provide you with a lot of ideas and advice on moving your initiation process to an ongoing model. But nothing here can bear fruit without first recognizing that the conversion process, by its very nature, is an individual journey. For this reason, we need to refocus on forming the person, not the group.

A Simple Solution That Doesn't Require Any Major Changes

Let's be honest. It's very difficult to change course midstream. And if you've made it this far through this book, you know that moving to an effective year-round process is going to take some time. But changing from a group process to an individual journey only requires a change in perspective, for you and for your seekers. And this can be done easily and quickly without disrupting what you may already have in place.

So how do you do this? Simple: Plan to meet one-on-one with each seeker (and their sponsor) in your process. This can also be a team effort, so spread the work around to the rest of the team. That way, it's not all on the initiation coordinator or director. Of course, make sure you meet with your team ahead of time to go over the ground rules and schedule a team meeting after to review how the sessions went.

Further, don't wait to do this. Even if you're only weeks away from Easter, why not take the time to meet with each seeker individually? I find almost every encounter with our seekers to be enlightening and inspiring. It reminds me why I've continued in this ministry for all these years—to hear their stories and their encounters with our living God. This meeting is also a way to help them through some difficult questions when it comes to our faith.

Planning these one-on-one meetings is *the* necessary starting point. This was the first step my predecessor took in her efforts to move us to an ongoing process, and I think you will be amazed, as was I, at how something this simple could serve as the catalyst for every other change we made along the way.

As for the structure of these meetings, I usually start by providing them with some discernment questions (examples of which can be found on the TeamRCIA web site) and giving them a couple of weeks to give the questions prayerful consideration before our meeting. This isn't some kind of assignment they have to turn in (there are never any tests or grades as part of the initiation process). This is just a tool for them to more easily enter into discernment. I also encourage them to write down their answers because writing helps the cognitive process. But writing is not a requirement, as not everyone is comfortable writing responses. These questions are only meant to serve as a jumping-off point for the discussion.

The meetings themselves should be scheduled for about an hour. They should be leisurely and conversational. They can be in your office, in a park, or in a café. This isn't an interview. Nor should it be a quick ten-minute review. Remember, depending on how your process has been running up to this point, your seekers may not have had the chance for this type of one-on-one conversation before, so gauge your approach accordingly. Nor should you or the seekers feel pressured to finish these conversations according to some deadline. If you have a large group, these individual meetings should be spaced out over a few weeks, giving you and them a chance to schedule them at your mutual convenience.

The most important part of these one-on-one conversations is understanding that this is not going to be a one-time thing. These meetings will be one of your primary tools throughout their entire stay in the process. Our getting to know the seekers and their getting to know us is one more way of bringing your seekers into community, not as "teacher and student" but as people and as individuals. This is how real communities are built and how we can help form the seekers into the greater parish community. Only by talking with them regularly can we help them see their progress through the process and discern their readiness for the next step on their journey.

The Importance of Building Community

When we think of building community within the initiation process, we often think of building community among our group of seekers—like a small church community or cohort. We need to expand our understanding of community.

When we talk of building community within the catechumenate, we need to think bigger. We need to think outside the box of our session space and consider what it means to be part of the larger parish community. The *Directory for Catechesis* reminds us that "[t]he Christian community is the primary agent of catechesis" (218). Becoming Catholic means embracing the dual nature of our faith. You cannot be Catholic without building a personal prayer life—a personal relationship with the Lord. But neither can you be Catholic and not be part of a community—an active and participating member of the parish community. Our faith takes both. It needs both.

I understand the draw of trying to form our initiation group into some kind cohort. Forming groups is part of our human and Christian nature. I've also seen where we want to protect our catechumens and candidates from any outside influences, like a mother hen protecting her chicks, not wanting them to fly the coop until they've been sufficiently prepared for the world beyond. But the truth is, shielding our seekers is both detrimental to their formation and to their faith journey.

Look, I get it. Parish is like family—all the good aspects of family as well as all the challenging aspects. Every parish family has the equivalent of that crazy aunt or uncle who is perhaps not the best representative of Christian love, and we feel the need to protect our precious seekers from these negative influences—at least until they've become more comfortable in their faith.

Our job as initiation catechists isn't to protect them from the parish community; it's to introduce them to the parish community. And this is how the parish becomes involved in the initiation process. I've worked with a number of catechists trying to figure out how we can get the community involved in the initiation process, but the answer was always staring us in the face. It's not how we can get the community involved in our initiation process; it's how those in the process need to be getting involved in the community, no matter how imperfect. After all, no community is perfect, just as none of us are perfect.

In chapter 2, I quoted *Gaudium et Spes*, reminding us that the church exists in and of this world. The same needs to apply to our initiation processes. We can't treat our seekers as if they're not yet part of the parish. The moment they join us they become part of the parish. Our job is to begin integrating them into parish life, beginning with Sunday Mass and extending out to everything else the parish has to offer them.

A Common Misconception about Adult Seekers

For too many years, for many reasons, we've pretty much operated our adult initiation processes from a "group" perspective,
with the assumption that everyone in the group had the same
starting point ("I know nothing about the Catholic faith") and
everyone had the same goals ("becoming a Catholic at the Easter
Vigil").

Time and experience, however, have taught us otherwise, show-
ing us that neither of these assumptions is true. Adult seekers
come to us with a variety of experiences, which affect both their
starting point and their goals in the initiation process. By discount-
ing that experience, we not only ignore their previous life and
faith experiences, we risk leading them down a path of initiation
that may not be appropriate, pastorally or canonically.

Adult Seekers Come with a Lifetime of Experience

Catechizing children in groups has traditionally been seen as
having a certain efficiency and perceived effectiveness, only because their age and grade level serves as a strong indicator of their
life experience. The same cannot be said for adults. The vast differences in age and life experiences they bring to our door requires
us to look beyond these assumptions. I would also argue that our
experiences with adult formation through the catechumenate have
helped us to recognize that our models for catechizing children
also need to be reexamined.

Our initiation process needs to begin with a more thorough time
for inquiry. Further, when it comes to the period of evangelization
and precatechumenate, I think we wrongly assume that we are a
neutral party in this endeavor. On the contrary, this first period is
a two-way street. It's not just for them to get to know us as church,
it's an opportunity for us to get to know each other as people.

Reinventing the Inquiry Process

Inquiry is not a group process. Nor should it be treated as an
academic introduction to the Catholic faith. At best, a group ap-

proach is pedantic, and at worst, it's insulting. We need to recognize that all those who come to us have already been touched by the Holy Spirit. They already have a sense of God, and more often than not, already know something about our faith and the church.

We cannot and should not make any assumptions about what the seekers do or do not know, nor what they have or have not experienced. Instead, we need to get to know them. The period of evangelization and precatechumenate is a one-on-one period of discovery for both the seeker and the initiation team. We get to know them and their needs, while they get to know who we are (as individuals, as a parish, and as a church). Through this exchange we both assess what it might take for them to be fully initiated into our Christian community.

So how do we reinvent the inquiry process? I could go into detail about how we developed this in our parish, but I find Nick Wagner's book *Seek the Living God: Five RCIA Inquiry Questions for Making Disciples* (Liturgical Press) provides a most useful and workable model. Perhaps the most important element of Wagner's approach is that it now places the burden of responsibility on the seeker, not the team. No longer are we pushing them through a course of study, but instead, we're guiding them on a journey where the timetable is set by them, not by us.

An Individual Journey Shared as a Group

So what of our traditional catechetical sessions? Just because everyone in the catechumenate is on their own personal journey doesn't mean they can't share part of that journey with everyone else in a group setting.

Put another way, the catechumenate is not a group of people on a singular journey, but rather, individuals sharing their own journeys with a group of others. It might sound like I'm saying the same thing, but there is a crucial difference, and that is one of perspective.

The seekers participating in catechetical sessions are not all traveling the same path—not the same spiritual path, nor the same ritual path. Their experiences are different, their motivations are different, and their goals are different. Similarly, every seeker needs to understand that this is not a group process. Their journey is unique, even though they are sharing part of that journey in group catechesis.

Catechetical Sessions Become Only Part of the Process

You may recall that we've previously recommended throwing out your syllabus in favor of sessions that follow the liturgy and the seasons of the church year. That's because our catechetical sessions don't make up the entire formation process. Instead, they are only part of it. Formation also occurs when they participate in Mass every week and participate in other activities in the life of the parish.

And because catechetical sessions follow along with the church year, individuals can more easily jump into and out of those sessions without the fear of "missing something important." Remember, for many seekers, their journey through the catechumenate may be a full year or more, while for others it may be less. There is no fixed timetable for this period of the process when you consider a seeker's previous experience and needs.

How Long Will It Take?

This is perhaps the number-one question I get from seekers. They think this is a simple question because they come in with certain expectations, made all the more difficult by the fact that this is how we in initiation ministry have portrayed the process for many years (and how some parishes still do).

In order to help them better understand our approach, I explain how Christian initiation is not a series of classes. It's an apprenticeship. It is a process of conversion to Christ. How long that takes must take into account many different factors based on the individual seeker's needs and goals, all of which are discovered as they go through the period of evangelization and precatechumenate.

Redefining When the Process Starts

It's no secret that life in many parishes follows the academic calendar. As fall approaches, many of our parish schools, groups, and ministries begin to awaken from their long summer slumber. For most every parish I've encountered, that includes adult faith formation and initiation.

The fact that adult initiation ministry tends to ramp up activity in the fall isn't necessarily a problem, but how we see it and how we announce it definitely can be. Here's a case in point. I've recently seen two different parish bulletin announcements. One read "RCIA classes begin on . . ." The other read, "Registration for RCIA starts on . . ." Let's unpack these announcements to see where the problems arise.

The first problem is how they both use the "RCIA" acronym, which those who have no experience of this ministry will likely not understand. I've seen some parishes try to resolve this by spelling out what the "Rite of Christian Initiation of Adults" is or means, which is helpful, but doesn't really get to the heart of the process (especially if those seekers don't fit into the actual rite, like baptized Catholics or Christians who have had some formation).

Next is the use the word "classes." This makes conversion to Christ sound like an academic exercise, which it is not. Becoming a Catholic shouldn't be like joining a club or completing a certificate program. It needs to be viewed as building a relationship with our living God—a life-long relationship—which is facilitated through active involvement in the Christian community.

Then there's my biggest problem: the use of words like "begin" or "start." Here again, we're giving both our seekers, the community, and us as initiation ministers a false impression of when the process actually begins. It doesn't start when *we* say it starts. It starts when the Holy Spirit calls that seeker to us. The initiation process begins with that first phone call or that first face-to-face inquiry. It doesn't begin with us, it begins with them, the seekers. Our initiation processes at every level need to recognize that the call to conversion can happen at any time, and we as ministers need to be prepared to receive them when they call, no matter when that call comes.

Now, I can see how some people might say that I'm making too much over the word "start." It's just a word. But imagine instead if you used the word "resume" instead of "begin" in these announcements. Pause and ask yourself what this small difference means. Outwardly, the word "resume" says that the catechumenate is a continuous and ongoing process, which it is. Inwardly, it reminds us that some catechumens and candidates who were not ready to be initiated or received at the previous Easter are continuing their journey.

Reallocating Resources to This New Paradigm

While an ongoing, year-round process demands that we reconsider when the process starts, we as team members also need to make sure we have our resources in the right places to respond. This doesn't necessarily mean finding more team members; it means reallocating the resources you already have to a different set of tasks. Most importantly, you want to have team members in place and ready to respond for when the Holy Spirit calls new seekers to your door, no matter what time of the year. The rest is just resuming a regular schedule of activities to keep them moving forward, wherever and whenever they enter that process.

Chapter 4

Treating Adults as Adults

Many of us working in initiation ministry have been around the church for a while. Some of us are lifelong Catholics, while others of us joined the church through the catechumenate process and perhaps never left this ministry. Regardless of how we got to where we are, most of us are comfortable with where we are in our faith and in our relationship with Christ. If I had to choose one word to describe typical initiation catechists, it's that we are "mature" in our faith.

But we need to be careful, because that "maturity" can lead us to think of our seekers as "immature," at least in matters regarding our Catholic faith. And that can be a problem if we're not conscious of it and don't give it due consideration as we develop our initiation processes. Put another way, we can tend to think of our seekers as "children" in matters of faith, and when we think of our seekers as immature, we can downshift into "elementary teacher mode" instead of maintaining the mode of an adult learning facilitator.

While many of our seekers may be immature in the ways of faith, we also need to recognize and respect that they can be very mature in many other ways (and perhaps even in other faith traditions). This being the case, we need to consciously adjust our thinking and our processes to accommodate that adult perspective. In short, we need to make sure we're treating adults like adults.

Recognizing Different Adult Learning Styles and Circumstances

Treating adults as adults begins by recognizing that adult learning styles differ greatly from those of children or adolescents. Adults need a sense of ownership in the learning process. They also need to see that the process fulfills their individual needs and goals in order to remain interested. And there's another very important fact that we can't ignore: unlike most children in catechesis, adult seekers want to be here.

When I first entered this ministry, having spent some years in youth catechesis, I discovered I needed a whole new playbook. It's tempting to fall back on those youth catechetical strategies because it's not hard to think of an adult seeker's faith experience being at a similar "immature" level. But that thinking is shortsighted. Not only are adult learning styles different from children's, but also experience levels vary greatly from person to person.

That's not to say you can't accomplish effective catechesis in a group setting. The difference here is that your sessions no longer need to focus on highly specific topics. Instead, adult sessions are focused on the bigger picture—the seasons, the readings, or current events—and how these topics reflect back on our faith.

Early on, I would get frustrated when the group would get me "off-topic" in our discussions. Educators would consider this to be an issue of poor classroom management. But remember, this isn't a classroom. And this process should never be viewed as a class. Instead, I grew to understand that these seeming interruptions were the Holy Spirit at work. I had accidentally stumbled onto what we now refer to as a "mystagogical" model for discussion, where we as catechists can connect those personal questions or moments or experiences to the various teachings, doctrines, and traditions of our Catholic faith.

I remember one session where I had prepared for a discussion on the sacrament of baptism. As the discussion was just getting started, one of our seekers asked about the nature of the Eucharist (is it really the Body and Blood of Christ?). I could have put that question on hold and told them that we would discuss this another time, but there was an earnestness in this seeker's question and that energy was quickly picked up by others in the group. This now became our topic of discussion. My agenda was put aside. Catechesis is still happening, but now it's based on their actual needs, not on what I perceive they need according to some fixed common schedule.

On a more practical level, we also need to remember that being an adult comes with all the adult baggage: work, school, children, family, and all the obligations that fall outside of the spiritual quest. While they need to know that the process will require them to make some sacrifices—making adjustments to their personal lives and schedules—we should never let seekers feel like they must make a choice between their personal obligations and attending a catechetical session. Even I, as a volunteer, may have to miss a session due to unexpected circumstances.

This is a far cry from when I started as team member. Back then, it was made quite clear that missing more than three sessions put a seeker's initiation in jeopardy and that if seekers wanted to become Catholic, they needed to do what was necessary to attend all our sessions regularly, according to our schedule. Their schedules were never even considered—the equivalent of "our way or the highway." In fact, we would go so far as to suggest that if our session schedule didn't work for them, they should find another parish (and we kept a list of other parishes and their catechumenate schedules with us). How welcoming is that?

I've always had a problem with that approach. While I believe that individuals looking to become Christians will need to make certain personal sacrifices to get there, who are we to determine what those sacrifices need to be?

We're all grown-ups here, and we understand that real life can sometimes get in the way. Missing a catechetical session should not be a deal-breaker when it comes to the seeker's faith journey. Instead, we should treat these moments as opportunities for growth, both for them and for us. We learn to be more flexible and accommodating, both as catechists and as church, while they learn by finding ways to weave their faith journey into their regular lives. Achieving the balance between faith and adult obligations is something we all have to do.

Most importantly, all these issues can be addressed by following good practice during the precatechumenate. This is where we develop with them a catechetical plan that the seeker is responsible for following. We become facilitators, mentors, coaches, and advisors. Instead of trying to keep the group on a fixed timetable, we help individuals manage their own pace and goals. Adult initiation is not a group but an individual process assisted by group catechesis.

Are We Catechizing for Knowledge or Understanding?

I know a lot of catechists who approach their ministry with all the zeal of foreign missionaries, especially when it comes to initiation. That was the feeling we all had in our catechumenate team when I first joined. Here was our chance to bring Christ to those who had never had any experience with our faith. This missionary zeal not only drove our team but also our entire approach to the process. The problem with this missionary zeal, however, is that we left out one very important part of our mission: the needs of the seekers themselves.

One of the common mistakes we made was that we looked at our catechumens and candidates like they were "blank slates." And even if we knew that they had some experience of church, we were eager to put that aside in favor of what we had to teach them. The reality, however, is that our seekers are anything but blank slates. We too easily forget that the "A" in "RCIA" stands for "adults," which means they come with a lifetime of experience (and, yes, some baggage). This isn't something to ignore or put aside. Rather, it is something we need to embrace. We need to get to know them as individuals and, through that, learn what it is they are seeking and how we can guide them to their goals.

If there's one thing I've learned as an adult catechist, it's that nothing is what you expect. Over the years I've observed that most seekers—the vast majority of them—already have a sense of God and some knowledge of our Catholic faith. In fact, it's that experience that has helped lead them to our door. We as catechists have to respect that and work with that.

Simplistic discussion topics like "Who is God?" or "Who is Jesus?" discount their knowledge and experience, especially if they've had some previous Christian religious formation. We see that many seekers have done a lot of research about our faith already. That means we should be taking an approach to catechesis that goes beyond just knowledge of our faith to one that also brings them understanding.

Belief (or acceptance) doesn't come from knowledge. It comes from understanding. For example: Catholics believe that Jesus rose from the dead. Now, chances are that many, if not most, of your adult non-Catholic seekers know this to be one of our beliefs. It's not something we necessarily need to teach them. What we do need to do, however, is to help them to understand why we believe what we believe, in this case, why the resurrection is so important to us. It is vitally important when working with adults to address less of the "what" and more of the "why," because it is through understanding that we come to belief.

The Pyramid of Acceptance or Belief

I've developed what I call the "pyramid of acceptance" or the "pyramid of belief." Knowledge is the foundation. Belief (or acceptance) is the peak. In between these two is the layer of "understanding" that needs to form the bulk of our adult catechesis. In this layer, we help adults understand why we believe what we believe. But as with everything, this can't just be with words. It must also flow from our actions—as catechists, parishioners, and church.

Now, in all fairness, there are a lot of different pyramid models out there (the most famous perhaps being Maslow's hierarchy of needs). Although my model may not be original, I've been able to develop more details as to how it works and can be applied to catechesis on a broader level. We need to ask ourselves what's more important: Teaching seekers all we know about the Catholic faith, or helping them understand why we believe what we believe?

A Scripture professor of mine once taught us an old Mennonite phrase: "God speaks to our condition." Put another way, God meets us where we are at—physically, mentally, and spiritually. Our job as catechists is to facilitate that meeting, but if we don't know where our seekers are at, then we become very poor guides. Knowledge of our faith is important, but seekers can only know what they are ready to understand. We need to rise up and meet them where they are and help them navigate their journey to understanding that leads them to acceptance and belief and to faith at an adult level. Most importantly, we help them meet Christ.

Building the Pyramid

Of course, there are many methods for meeting the needs of our seekers, so we as catechists need to avail ourselves of those methods and practices that best benefit our adult learners. We also need to remember that our goal isn't just to teach them but to bring them the Gospel—to bring them to Christ. The *Directory for Catechesis* tells us:

> Catechesis does not have a single method, but is open to evaluating different methods, engaging in pedagogy and didactics, and allowing itself to be guided by the Gospel necessary for recognizing the truth of human nature. (195)

I had thought initially that the pyramid of belief model was just for adult learners, observing that children tended to skip the

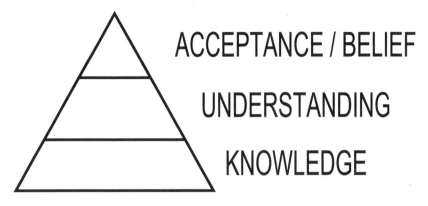

"understanding" layer and go directly from knowledge to acceptance. Think about preparing second-graders for their First Communion—at "the age of reason" (though you will forgive me if I mention that modern science has suggested that the brain isn't fully developed until our early twenties). We give them the knowledge that the bread and the wine are in fact changed into the Body and Blood of Christ, and that is enough for them to accept or believe.

After some more study and consideration, however, I came to realize that kids don't skip over the "understanding" layer; they just go through it with greater ease than most adults. That is accomplished with what I term "trust tunnels."

How is it that a child seems to accept our Catholic beliefs far more readily than someone who is older? It's because it is being presented by someone they trust: a parent, teacher, catechist, priest, deacon, religious, or some other "trusted" emissary or authority in their lives. They accept the message because they trust and accept the messenger.

But what happens when we mature? These earlier trust tunnels begin to break down because our trust in the messenger begins to breakdown. As adolescents begin to develop their own reasoning skills, critical thinking, logic, and executive functions, they begin to question what they once trusted and need to build their own understanding, rather than simply relying on what they are

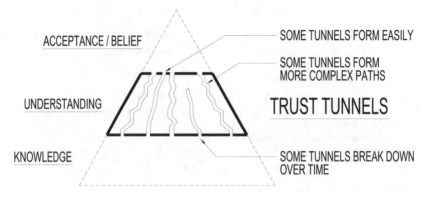

ACCEPTANCE / BELIEF — SOME TUNNELS FORM EASILY

SOME TUNNELS FORM
MORE COMPLEX PATHS

UNDERSTANDING — TRUST TUNNELS

KNOWLEDGE — SOME TUNNELS BREAK DOWN
OVER TIME

told. Further, as old trust relationships begin to get tested, new trust relationships develop, and because reasoning and critical thinking come into play, those newer trust relationships face much different tests than those from their childhood.

As adults, we still develop certain trust relationships. For example, when I wanted to develop my own skills in initiation ministry, I put my trust in a few national trainers whose experience is greater than my own. But that trust wasn't born overnight. It developed out of my having read their work, participated in training workshops, and seen for myself through our own processes at the parish that what they had to say was, in fact, trustworthy. In other words, they earned my trust, which over time allowed me to more readily accept what they have to say, even if sometimes I need to think about it for a while and work it through my own mental processes. All our relationships as adults require this mental exercise. This is why it takes time to build trust. The stronger that trust, the more resilient it becomes and, for seekers, the more easily they will understand the knowledge we provide through their encounters with Christ.

We face the same challenges every time we meet and work with our seekers, catechumens, and candidates. And while our love and passion for our faith (and for them) can help build that trust, we still need to recognize that they are still putting us and our beliefs to the test. They need to know not just *what* we believe but understand *why* we believe it. This will help build both their trust in us and in what we're sharing with them. And of course, by visibly practicing what we preach in the community, we enhance that trust.

As catechists, we tend to fall back on giving knowledge because it is quicker and easier to impart. Helping someone develop understanding, however, tends to be a much slower process. And that's okay. Not only do our seekers need to chew on this themselves for a while, but everyone processes information and experiences differently. Fortunately, the early Christian community and those who developed the current catechumenate process understood this, which is why paragraph 76 of the rite reminds us that "[t]he duration of the catechumenate will depend on the grace of God and on various circumstances." This time frame isn't driven by us imparting knowledge. It is driven by the catechumens developing understanding, which eventually leads to acceptance, which leads us all to God—on their schedule, not ours.

Chapter 5

Embracing Mystagogy

A while back I was talking with a group of initiation catechists from another parish (something I highly encourage on a regular basis). I was learning about their process, and they were asking me about ours. During this dialogue, one of the catechists asked me how often we used videos. I had to pause to think for a moment, which created a somewhat longer-than-expected silence. Eventually I said, "Almost never," to which I got a sort of stunned silence in response, like they couldn't comprehend what I had said. This opened a whole new avenue of discussion.

Now, don't get me wrong. I don't want to completely demonize the use of videos and PowerPoints, but I do believe there's a proper time and place for their use. When it comes to our regular catechetical sessions, a minimalist approach is best. Allow me to explain.

The Personal Approach

Earlier in this book, I noted that we need to focus on the individual, not the group. That includes employing a personal approach in our catechetical sessions. As catechists, we want to facilitate discussion and personal interaction: a dialogue. Only through dialogue does understanding begin to develop. Videos and PowerPoints, by their very nature, tend to be monologues—one-way conversations. While videos and PowerPoints can provide some excellent information with high quality production values, it's still just a lecture where we end up talking "at" them instead of talking "with" them.

Engaging through Discussions, Not Presentations

If you haven't guessed by now, I'm a big fan of the Socratic method of teaching, developed by the great teacher and philosopher Socrates from the fifth century BCE. Here, we engage the group with questions and active dialogue that help to stimulate critical thinking. Translating that into catechetical language and practice, it would be taking a *mystagogical* approach. Remember, we're not trying to teach them the Christian faith; we're assisting in their conversion to the Christian life. We're not just imparting knowledge; we're sharing our passion for Christ and his church.

Embracing a Mystagogical Approach

When initiation catechists talk about mystagogy, we have a tendency to focus on that fourth and final stage of the process, the period of post-baptismal catechesis or mystagogy. But mystagogy isn't just a point on the initiation journey. It is a process for providing catechesis that connects our encounters with Christ, primarily in the liturgy, to their significance for faith and meaning for our lives. It's a method that should be employed throughout the catechumenate.

As a catechetical approach, mystagogy is a process that asks us to look back at moments and events to see where Christ has been active in our lives. We look not just for big moments, but everyday moments. We try to see God in the ordinary. For our seekers, this discernment of the way God is present in their daily lives becomes an invaluable formation tool, allowing them to see and become closer to God. One seeker I worked with was having trouble coming to a decision about changing jobs. She told me that she had prayed on it but hadn't found any guidance. She also mentioned an encounter with another friend who provided her some advice seemingly unrelated to her job issue. As she was explaining this, I could see how there might be a connection. So I asked her, could it be that God was speaking to you through your friend? It wasn't something she had ever considered. She was so set on finding God in a "burning bush" that she wasn't able to see that the answer could be right in front of her. It was a chance for her to see that God was in fact with her.

If we limit the mystagogical process to the scrutinies or the time after initiation, we're too late. If we truly believe that it was the action of the Holy Spirit that brought the seekers to our door, we owe it to them to help them see this for themselves as early and as often as possible. This is further supported by the *Directory for Catechesis*:

> The Christian's formative journey, as attested to the mystagogical catechesis of the Church Fathers, always had an experiential character, but never neglecting the understanding of the faith. The living and persuasive encounter with Christ proclaimed by authentic witnesses was critical. (97)

This formation isn't limited to what they might have experienced from a liturgy or other parish activities, but includes everyday activities. Our experience of God isn't limited to the walls of the church.

Curating Your Videos and PowerPoints Carefully

As I said, videos are helpful if used properly. There are some that can cover a topic with far more insight and understanding than I can provide. But too often, they can become a crutch—something we fall back on out of convenience or our own perceived lack of knowledge. I recommend picking one or two that really work for you and dumping the rest. And always leave plenty of time for discussion after. No videos should be presented without sufficient time for discussion. Like any topic where we use the mystagogical approach, we need time to connect what they've just seen in the video to their everyday lives and their experiences of Christ.

Also, make sure to curate your video topics to your audience. If seekers have a hard time connecting the video with their lived experience of Christ, it can fall on deaf ears and closed minds. Also, consider that we're not trying to turn our seekers into theologians. We're simply trying to bring them closer to Christ. A video describing the intricacies of the paschal mystery might leave your seekers scratching their heads or falling asleep. On the other hand, I've seen videos that describe the structure of the Mass with such poetry that it will make you rush out and participate in the next available Mass. The videos we do choose need to leave our seekers with a sense of wonder and awe that we could never provide by just a table discussion. Videos need to enhance your discussion. The one or two you might use over the course of a year need to be suited to the task of bringing our seekers to Christ, not to the seminary.

As for PowerPoints, we also need to be careful that we're not overusing them. There are some topics where graphics and bullet points can be extremely helpful. But again, this should be the exception, not the rule. As with my caveat regarding videos, my objection to the excessive use of PowerPoints (or other similar slide presentations) is that it can move a dialogue to a monologue. PowerPoints work well for classroom lectures and workshop presentations because those activities require imparting a certain amount of knowledge within a set time frame. That's not our goal, which is not so much the transfer of knowledge but the development of understanding required to bring seekers to belief.

We also need to embrace the opportunities that a year-round process has to offer. Here, there is no pressure to impart a certain curriculum of knowledge within a limited time frame. The period of the catechumenate is sufficiently and accordingly long enough for each seeker such that there's plenty of time for them to discover the important aspects of our Catholic faith. These flow from the journey through the liturgical year and the celebration of the seasons. Remember also that topics of discussion are best presented when they connect with the regular life of the parish.

So, similar to curating your videos, make an effort to curate your PowerPoints. Pick only a handful where they really work best. Use of PowerPoints and videos should be the exception, not the rule.

Making Room for the Holy Spirit

Traditionally, we catechists have spent a lot of time planning and preparing for our sessions, and like many catechists, you might feel like there's never enough time to cover everything you want to cover. Unfortunately, the pressure to "stick to the script" can force out the movement of the Holy Spirit.

There have been more than a few occasions where I've ended up chucking my entire plan for our session because the table's discussion turned in a different direction. Was mystagogy still happening? Yes. Was catechesis still happening? Yes. Then, regardless of the plan I had, the session was a success!

Perhaps one of the hardest lessons I've learned as an initiation catechist was that my plan may not be God's plan. So rather than fight that, I learned to work with it. By dumping your established syllabus for a liturgically based process and by building flexibility into your session plans, you make room for the Holy Spirit. Remember, being open year-round means you get to play the long game. You don't have to feel pressured to cover "x" number of topics within "x" number of weeks.

Much Ado about Doing the RCIA Online

It is an unfortunate reality of our computer age that much of our communication is no longer performed face to face. In fact, younger generations often avoid phone calls altogether, communicating instead through text messages and social media.

While we as church must find ways to engage with seekers (and each other) through these various platforms, there remains nothing better than engaging with people face to face. After all, this is what Jesus did. Jesus didn't write lessons on parchment or have scribes copy and send them out to neighboring communities. Jesus walked to those communities, met with those people, and delivered his message with words and actions. Jesus didn't take the easy way out—and as initiation minsters, neither should we, no matter how tempting that might be.

For example, I got a phone call once from someone asking about doing the catechumenate online. This isn't the first time I've been asked this question or been shown resources that make initiation look like an online learning program. How should we respond to these situations? I remind these seekers that the purpose of Christian initiation is to enter a process of conversion, not attend a series of classes. The goal isn't to complete a course of study; it's to grow in a relationship with Christ through active participation in the parish community.

The Initiation Process Is an Apprenticeship

While an apprentice must learn certain facts about their trade to be successful, the key to mastering that trade relies on continual practice—actually doing the work. The good apprentice follows the master's instructions and imitates the master's methods. The master also knows that the apprentice must ease into the trade. A good master won't try to teach them everything all at once, but instead, teach them gradually.

The good master carefully assesses their abilities, giving them appropriate tasks at first, and once those tasks are mastered, moving on to the more difficult challenges. This is also the initiation process. We guide them through the path of the process—the period of evangelization and precatechumenate, the catechumenate, the period of purification and enlightenment, and finally, the period of mystagogy. And even then, once they've been through this process, we recognize that none of these neophytes will succeed without continuing to practice the faith. Initiation isn't the end but a transitional moment of a lifelong faith journey.

Those of us in initiation ministry need to take this idea of apprenticeship to heart. Not only that, we need to put it into practice and profess it to our parish communities. Here we are often our own worst enemies, especially when our programs look more like classroom lessons instead of using mystagogy and active participation in the community as a model for catechesis.

Having All Your Seekers around the Same Table

Perhaps one of the most common questions I hear when moving to an ongoing year-round process is, "Do we need to break everyone up into separate groups to facilitate the preparation process?" In other words, do we keep together certain cohorts who may be on a similar path? Or do we keep cohorts who "started" together in a separate group? These are all fair questions, but in the light of moving to an ongoing process, the concern about separate groups is really a nonissue.

The key lies in separating the rites and the ritual path from the catechetical process. Not everyone in the group needs to be on the same ritual path in order to be enriched by a group catechetical session. And since session topics don't follow a prescribed syllabus, the discussion can benefit all the seekers around the table, regardless of their ritual or catechetical paths.

There is both a spiritual and a practical benefit to this approach. On the practical side, most initiation teams are stretched far enough having to maintain one group, let alone trying to form a separate team for each cohort or group on a similar path.

In smaller parishes especially, where you may have a small team and only a handful of seekers, there is little value in trying to break them up into even smaller groups. On the spiritual side, the benefit lies in allowing seekers to see that everyone, both within the group of seekers or within the entire parish community, is on a separate path. Not everyone has had the same experiences. Not everyone has the same spiritual or sacramental needs. Yet with all these differences, we somehow form a church. The thing that binds us together is Christ, not whatever sacrament we're preparing for, not our level of catechetical learning. It is the same Spirit that calls each seeker to the table.

Some might have difficulty with this new approach to group catechesis. After all, we've learned that the basic tenets of academic instruction and group dynamics lie in the idea of everyone having a common experience and a common goal. But experience has shown this is a nonissue.

First, you can't count on a group of adult seekers to have either a common experience or a common sacramental need. Next, and more importantly, we're all adults. I have found once they understand the nature of the process, our seekers adjust easily to the flexible dynamics of the group setting, so long as the actual catechesis followed a more mystagogical process. That is, we let our common experience as a church community guide us into seeing how Christ has intervened in our lives—through the celebration of the liturgical seasons, through the celebration of Mass, and through the various activities and events of the ongoing life of the parish.

The key to a successful catechetical session isn't how much information about the Catholic faith is dispensed; it's in seeing Christ through the eyes of everyone around the table. Catechists don't need to prepare a lesson. They need to facilitate the ongoing discussion—a discussion that can benefit everyone around the table, from the most senior catechist to the least catechized seeker. We can all learn from each other.

Being Flexible—Lessons Learned from the Pandemic

Sometimes it takes a crisis to snap us out of our complacency. The COVID-19 crisis forced many of us to rethink not only how we deliver on our adult formation processes but how we can deliver the necessary rites while remaining socially distant. Many of us were forced to try things we never thought possible. We needed to go beyond our comfort zones, and many of us came up with some very creative solutions along the way. We proved that church can continue even when faced with unprecedented circumstances.

Unfortunately, once a crisis passes, there's a lot of pressure to "get back to normal." In many ways, that means those creative and effective solutions get left behind as we fall back into old habits. This isn't just related to initiation ministry; it's a phenomenon all organizations face. There's also another hard truth many organizations learned through the COVID-19 crisis—that the challenges brought about by the crisis only accelerated certain trends that were already present. For us as church, that meant recognizing that our overall membership is on a steep decline and that many of the processes we followed in forming both our youth and adults need to evolve. The need for this evolution has long been known, and the publishing of the new *Directory for Catechesis* does help us to see where we as church need to go with regards to formation and evangelization.

Much of what we talk about in this book relates to rethinking how we implement our initiation processes to bring them more in line with the spirit and intent of the rite and the *Directory for Catechesis*.

Let what we've learned through this crisis remind you of what's possible so that you're not anxious to fall back to "the way it was." Instead, take this as a sign from the Holy Spirit that change can be a necessary good. Far too often, what makes us unable to change is our own aversion to change. For years now, we've seen that an ongoing year-round model can lead to better discipleship, while making our jobs as initiation ministers much easier. The flexibility we learned during the COVID-19 crisis needs to carry on well beyond the crisis and remain an integral part of our processes.

Chapter 6

The Fork in the Road:
Some Common Misconceptions,
Ours and Theirs

We all have certain expectations when it comes to adult initiation. Seekers also have certain built-in expectations, including preconceived notions that all they need to do is take some classes and celebrate their sacraments on a given date. And to be fair, we catechists have operated under those same expectations for many years (and some of us still do). As initiation catechists, we've been exploring the road ahead to an ongoing year-round process that breaks that academic model for one that builds better discipleship. It's a major change for us as church, and it means having to address certain misconceptions about the adult initiation process.

Misconception 1:
Everyone Follows a School Year Schedule

It's no secret that the vast majority of parishes tend to follow an academic-style calendar year—not just for catechetical and initiation ministries but for many other parish activities. Part of this is the result of many parishes having their own schools and many parishioners having school-aged children. Whatever the reason (and there are many), parish life for most of us tends to follow an academic calendar where most everything shuts down during the summer. The problem is, we so easily conform to that kind of schedule as catechists that we lose sight of those seekers and parishioners who are not married to an academic calendar.

The reality is that many adult seekers (and parishioners) are not confined to an academic schedule. Unless they have children in school or work for a school themselves, the academic calendar means little to them.

We need to recognize that not everyone is tied to an academic schedule—or for that matter, a Monday through Friday schedule. As initiation ministers who work with adults, we need to respond to their needs, even if their calling comes during the summer months. We need people and processes in place to address those needs so that we never have to tell a seeker, "Come back in the fall."

Further, what might seem to be a burden to us as a team is actually an opportunity. There are many adults in our parishes eager to do something during the summer or to continue with their ministries during this time. Find them and work with them to provide outlets for seekers looking to join. At the very least, Sunday Mass is still always happening, so pair up seekers with parishioners who can accompany them. You will be amazed at the amount of catechesis that can come from this weekly Mass participation.

Misconception 2: We Have to Teach Them Everything about the Catholic Faith

First of all, we need to recognize the absurdity of that concept. No one person can know *everything* about the Catholic faith. Even for those of us who may know more than the average Catholic, there are still many things to learn. And that's OK. It's the nature of the Body of Christ. We all have our own gifts from the Spirit, and we are all on a journey that is constantly evolving and growing.

That said, the rite does state:

> The instruction that the catechumens receive during this period
> [of the catechumenate] should be of a kind that while presenting
> Catholic teaching in its entirety also enlightens faith, directs the
> heart toward God, fosters participation in the liturgy, inspires
> apostolic activity, and nurtures a life completely in accord with
> the spirit of Christ. (78)

In my experience, many of our catechetical processes focus too
much on the first part of this paragraph (presenting Catholic teaching in its entirety) rather than on the remainder of that paragraph
(directing the heart toward God). Too many of our catechetical
processes look more like advanced theology studies than basic
Christian teaching. We also have a tendency to over-deliver on
the requirement of presenting Catholic teaching in its entirety
while overlooking the fact that Catholic teaching is fully presented
both in our Creed, the liturgical seasons, and the celebration of
Mass over a period of time.

Additionally, we also have to consider that directive from paragraph 78 in light of what paragraph 120 says regarding their readiness for the Rite of Election, that "catechumens are expected to
have undergone a conversion in mind and in action and to have
developed a sufficient acquaintance with Christian teaching as
well as a spirit of faith and charity."

Paragraph 120 is pivotal for our understanding of a seeker's
readiness to be initiated! It doesn't focus on Catholic teaching so
much as it focuses on "conversion in mind and in action," which
means that they're heading in the right direction. Further, it tells
us that what they need is a "sufficient acquaintance with Christian
teaching, as well as a spirit of faith and charity." Here again we
tend to focus more on "teaching" than we do on building a "spirit
of faith and charity."

As initiation catechists, we need to stop overthinking the teaching aspect of the process and trust that they are being sufficiently
exposed to the teachings of the church through their active participation in the church. This only works, however, if we throw

away our syllabuses and timetables, letting each participant's journey have the time it needs to unfold. Also remember, we're not charged with turning seekers into theologians; we're charged with helping them become true disciples.

Misconception 3: We Have to Keep to a Tight Schedule if We're Going to Get Everyone Through

I've seen it (and done it) where we take a calendar for the next year, mark the date for the Easter Vigil, and work our way back to develop a schedule of catechesis and activities that should allow us to "cover everything" in time for Easter. The trouble is, we're applying the wrong tool for the wrong reasons. This kind of "backdating" is a great tool for project planning. But here's the thing. Initiation is not a "project." It's a "process." Any sort of backdating like this is the antithesis of the spirit of the catechumenate.

The reality is that the Easter Vigil is an arbitrary date we set for ourselves, and in doing so, we end up making the Vigil the focus of our catechetical process. Instead, we need to be focusing on the journey—*their* journey, on their schedule, not ours—a journey that is as individual as they are, but one that needs to be integrated into the life of the parish and the liturgical cycle.

Put another way, seekers should not be seen as students looking toward graduation; they should be seen as apprentices who must discern when they are ready for the next step in their process—a process that may or may not include the Easter Vigil.

Misconception 4: If We Go to a Year-Round Process, We Have to Run Sessions All Year

It never fails. Whenever I talk with fellow RCIA catechists about our ongoing year-round process, I inevitably get the question, "Does that mean you run your sessions all year round?"

Running a year-round process does not mean you have to run catechetical sessions all year round. There is nothing in the rite that directs us to have catechetical sessions every week. The catechumenate process doesn't revolve around a calendar or a schedule;

it revolves around the people in the process. Nor does the process happen only in the room where you host your catechetical sessions; it also happens in the pews every week at Mass. It happens at various parish events and gatherings. It happens whenever our catechumens and candidates take part in the full and active life of our parish communities.

Now that doesn't minimize the value or importance of having catechetical sessions, but what it does allow is freedom and flexibility for how you schedule your sessions. Even if you have held weekly sessions traditionally, you likely took breaks from that schedule around the holidays or during the summer. That doesn't necessarily need to change.

What you do need to consider is whether your schedule of sessions is meeting the needs of the seekers. For example, my parish serves both a community college and a large university. Many of our seekers' lives revolve around these institutions, so we schedule our catechetical sessions around their calendars. I have also seen success with a "block" schedule, where we meet for sessions weekly for six to eight weeks, then take a week or two off.

Another challenge is what to do during the summer. Here again, I have always looked to the needs of the seekers and the parish. While some of our seekers would be away for the summer, we would have others who were around and wanted to do something. Not having weekly sessions doesn't mean you have to shut down entirely—you just do something different.

In my parish, in addition to Sunday Mass, we've done movie nights, field trips to the cathedral, field trips to historical sites, mini-retreats or days of prayer, day hikes—there's any number of activities that you can do. We would even open these to the rest of the parish or do them in conjunction with other parish groups. Catechesis doesn't just happen in a catechetical session.

Misconception 5: The Catechumenate Is a Series of Classes You Take to Become Catholic

It is scary to think how common this idea is among our seekers, our parishioners, and even some of our catechists. If you've made it to this part of the book, you understand that the catechumenate is not an academic process but an apprenticeship. But if we're ever going to change the habits and minds of those we serve, I can't express enough the importance of expunging academic language from our lexicon.

To some it might seem trivial. To others it might seem like political correctness run amok. But as I have said before, the words we use are important. The story of creation and the opening to John's Gospel remind us that words matter.

If we are to change the language around the initiation process, we must lead that charge. Not only do we need to be watchful of the words we use, but we need to catechize others—our fellow catechists, our parish staffs, our parishioners, and sometimes, yes, even our pastors.

So while it might seem like a minor thing, the words we use can have a significant impact. And once we explain why it's important to avoid academic language as it relates to our initiation processes, it becomes easier for all of us to understand and adapt.

Misconception 6: Father Knows Best

As Catholics in ministry, we have a tendency to "defer to Father" when it pertains to just about anything. After all, your pastor is the final authority because pastors bear the responsibility on behalf of the community. We also have a tendency to turn to Father because we see him as the expert in all things having to do with faith. But here's the truth—priests are people too, and, like all people, they have all been graced differently by the Holy Spirit. They are not, in fact, the experts on all things. No priest could be. And not only that, our pastors in particular have much more to do and worry about.

Some priests and deacons have a lot of experience and expertise in adult faith formation and initiation ministry. Many, however, do not. This is why our own training is so important. More and more of our pastors rely on us, their lay ministers, to take care of things on their behalf. And oftentimes we may find ourselves in the position of catechizing them on the finer aspects of this ministry.

When working with your pastor, you need to get to know them. Just as we do with our own seekers, we need to sit down with them and talk with them. We need to be engaging with them on a regular basis. Only then can we build trust, our trust in them and their trust in us.

Managing Expectations

These are just a few of the common misconceptions I've encountered during my time in this ministry. Chances are that each of you have your own experiences when it comes to facing any number of misconceptions about the catechumenate. All this falls under the topic of "managing expectations."

Some people come to us with specific expectations. Others come to us with very few because they don't know enough about the process. Regardless, the key to addressing any expectations is to identify them and address them up front or as soon as possible. Only then can we prevent any misunderstandings or misconceptions.

Chapter 7

Wash, Rinse, Repeat?

I got the name for this chapter from the often-quoted line from the instructions on the back of a bottle of shampoo. And for those of you who think this old trope is apocryphal, I challenge you to look at the instructions on the back of your own shampoo bottles. I checked those in my home, and though not exact, I did find some form of these instructions on all of them.

Most of us probably think such instructions are not needed for a bottle of shampoo. But when you consider this more deeply, we need to recognize that not all of us share a common experience. We may live in a world where shampoo is common and its use is taught to us from a very early age. But that's just from our own point of view. Many others in the world may not share that perspective. To put this in more catechetical terms, we need to be conscious of our own "hermeneutic."

Much has been said and written about cultural awareness and cultural sensitivity, with the recognition that we have our own personal experiences and biases. Those biases can lead us to a form of insensitivity toward others, especially those whose experiences are different from our own. There's the well-known proverb that says, "Never judge someone until you've walked a mile in their shoes." Though this proverb doesn't come explicitly from the Bible, its ideal of not judging others is a common thread running through many of the Scriptures and is completely compatible with our Catholic teaching.

What does this mean for us for our initiation ministry? Quite simply, we need to recognize we have a tendency to let our own biases and experiences drive our initiation processes. Put another way, just because "we've always done it this way" doesn't mean it's the only way or the best way. As Jesus instructed the rich man (Matt 19:16-22), maintaining the status quo is not enough. The point of that particular story in Matthew's Gospel wasn't so much a condemnation of the man's wealth but a call to one's need for continuing conversion.

Falling into a Rhythm Can Build a False Sense of Effectiveness

The other problem with the "wash, rinse, repeat" approach is that it can lead to complacency about your initiation process—"If it ain't broke, don't fix it." Very often, we get so much into a rhythm with our catechetical and sacramental preparation processes that we become too comfortable. We see people entering the process, going through the process, and completing the process. But are we keeping track of them after they complete the process? Are they staying active in the community?

More importantly, how can we improve our initiation processes so that we're not just pushing people through the motions but are actually creating disciples for Christ?

Earlier, I referenced one of my favorite passages from the Second Vatican Council's *Gaudium et Spes*, the Pastoral Constitution on the Church in the Modern World: "[We must now] consider the presence of the church in the world, and its life and activity there" (40).

I bring it up again here to ask the question: Is your process changing with the needs of your community? How has your community changed over the years? Is your initiation process helping your community grow?

We can't just "wash, rinse, repeat."

In order to make sure our initiation process is remaining effective, both in meeting the needs of the parish and in developing an ongoing year-round process, I recommend following a different set of instructions:

1. Develop your plan.

2. Implement your plan.

3. Evaluate your plan.

This isn't a one-time exercise. In order to be effective, it needs to be an ongoing activity, not just for the initiation director and the team, but for all those responsible for implementing the catechumenate. That would include:

- Your pastor

- Any associate pastors

- Your deacon(s)

- Your director of formation

- Your liturgy team (liturgy director, music director, lectors, other ministers)

- Representatives of parish groups (Bible study, social outreach, prayer group, etc.)

This is not a definitive list, but it's a starting point. The goal here is to include a good cross section of the parish leadership, remembering that this process "takes place within the community" (RCIA 4).

First Stop: Develop Your Plan

A plan must first begin with a vision. What is your vision for your parish adult initiation process? Think about that. Pray on that. Write it down. Now, here's the harder part: What is the vision your other team members or stakeholders have? Plans often fail because not all the stakeholders share the same vision, which can cause frustration and discord—and can actually undermine the planning process. That's because everyone is aiming at a different target, working toward different goals.

And don't be afraid to have a grand vision. While a grand vision might seem impossible to achieve, it does need to be the guiding light for the next part of developing your plan—identifying the steps necessary to get to your vision.

You may be familiar with the question, "How do you eat an elephant?" The answer is: one bite at a time. Too often, people will downsize their vision to fit what they see as obstacles. There will be challenges, but the key is to identify them—these become the action steps of your plan. You may need to find a way around or through some of these challenges, but the vision remains the same—it just might take a few more bites of that elephant to achieve. So separate those goals that are short-term and long-term. Put them on a calendar or schedule so you know which elements are going to be implemented and when. This may change down the road, but write them down and give them a date for implementation.

Second Stop: Implement Your Plan

Next is putting the plan into action. I've worked with some people who would say this is the hardest part, but I have a secret. Implementing the plan is easier than developing the plan, but only if you do your homework, only if you do enough work on the planning phases, and only if you've engaged your stakeholders early and gotten consensus and buy-in on the plan.

That's not to say that you won't encounter problems as you implement your plan. Some problems are foreseeable. For those, your plan should include a "plan B" alternative. But there are also obstacles that are unforeseeable. These often are things outside your control, like what we saw with the COVID-19 pandemic. What we learned during the pandemic was the need to be flexible.

Oftentimes the need to do things differently offers us creative solutions, and sometimes those creative solutions can become tools we keep in our toolbox to be used regularly. One such tool for many is the use of Zoom or other online platforms for meetings or sessions or other activities. While holding these activities in person has always been the preferred method, that doesn't mean we should completely abandon use of virtual platforms. Under certain circumstances this tool can be very convenient, efficient, and valuable.

Third Stop: Evaluate Your Plan

You can have the best plan in the world, and implementing that plan may have been a breeze, but if you don't take the time to evaluate your plan, you're courting trouble! This third stop, evaluating your plan, is the step that most organizations and businesses tend to skip. Don't! Schedule some time to gather everyone together and do an analysis of your progress.

There are all sorts of tools you can use for evaluating your process, but I'm going to recommend a method called "start, stop, continue."

> **Start:** Looking over the past year and how your process went during that year, ask yourself: What was missing? What should you start doing that you weren't doing? Perhaps it's something simple like, "We should start opening our catechetical sessions with a prayer," or "We should start holding some of our sessions outside when the weather is nice." You can also use the "start" step to introduce an improvement to your process. For example, "We should start having more one-on-one follow-up sessions with our seekers to see how they're doing through the process," or "We should start having our sponsors accompany our seekers to Mass every week."
>
> **Stop:** These are those things that you want to stop doing. For example, "We should stop starting our sessions late," or "We

should stop having our sessions get out late." Stop is also a chance to look at bigger aspects of your process that should be examined: "We should stop using so many PowerPoints," or "We should stop having our sessions in a classroom."

Continue: These are those things that are going well with your process which you would like to continue doing. For example: "We should continue having a retreat day during Lent," or "We should continue having everyone bring a snack they can share during our break." Not only is this an opportunity to recognize those things you've done well over the past year, but it helps end the evaluation on a high note.

Make sure you write down each of these comments so you have a record of the evaluation. Also, you can use your previous year's evaluations as a starting point for this year's evaluation. Did you actually start what you wanted to start? Did you stop what you wanted to stop? Did you continue what you wanted to continue?

The goal of the evaluation is to make sure your process is remaining effective for your community, keeping in mind that the needs of the community change over time. Too often, we plan our processes in a vacuum, as we fail to notice that the world and our parish is changing around us. Is there something we should be doing differently? Should we change the time or day we meet for our sessions? Should we have sessions every other week? Are we missing an opportunity by not having activities during the summer? Most importantly, is what we're doing effective for where our community is today? What worked five, ten, or twenty years ago may not be effective today. Always be open to alternatives so you can be more responsive to the needs of your seekers and your community.

Remember

The goal of all this planning and evaluation is so that we remember—remember what we've done, remember what we want to do, and remember those whom we serve. I think these words from the *Directory for Catechesis* also help us in our efforts here:

> Memory is an integral dimension of salvation history. The people of Israel are constantly urged to keep memory alive, not to forget the Lord's benefits. (201)

As we lead our seekers to Christ, we should always take time to evaluate where we've been, where we are, and how best to continue spreading the Gospel.

Chapter 8

Getting Your Parish Involved in the Process

As Catholics, we've become comfortable with "silos"—those groups within the parish with whom we identify and spend most of our extracurricular time. These could be the choir, the Knights of Columbus, or Bible study—whatever group it is. This can be even more pronounced in those parishes that have bilingual or multilingual communities, with each primary language group operating like their own parish within a parish. And rarely do these silos come together. Usually, it takes a special event, like a parish anniversary or the annual fair, to bring these different silos together.

That's not to say that silos are entirely bad. The Spirit has given each of us different talents and capabilities, and it's natural to fall in with those ministries and activities and groups to which we've been drawn. The problem is that when it comes to the catechumenate, all these different silos have a role to play in the formation of our seekers. In fact, so does every person in the church. Unfortunately, no one has explained this very clearly to our parishioners, so it's up to us as initiation ministers (along with our pastors) to tell them.

During his general audience on May 22, 2013, Pope Francis reminded us that "evangelizing is the church's mission. It is not the mission of only a few, but it is mine, yours, and our mission."

Spreading the Word to the Rest of the Parish

So how do we remind the rest of the parish that they play an active, evangelical role in the initiation process? After all, many of our parishioners will be hearing this for the first time.

The parish plays an active role in the catechumenate by their participation in the rites during Mass. That may be true and liturgically accurate, but my bet is few parishioners understand this point. Nor is this the level of awareness or involvement we're looking for from our parishioners in their role as evangelizers. So it must take a concerted and coordinated effort with the pastor and other parish leaders to get the word out and help the people understand that they have a role in the formation of our catechumens and candidates.

This isn't something that can be done with a bulletin announcement or in a homily. While these are tried and true tools we should use, it needs to be much more. We need to leverage all the communication tools and platforms at our disposal. These include:

- Parish bulletin

- Homilies

- Announcements during Mass

- Online newsletters

- Email

- Parish social media (Instagram, Facebook, Twitter, Tik-Tok, etc.)

- Announcements at gatherings of various parish groups

- Banners and bulletin boards

- A retreat or day of prayer

With the cooperation of your pastor, your pastoral leadership team, and all the other stakeholders, you can present a consistent message reminding everyone that we all play a role in evangelization and in the initiation process. What is that role? To walk with our seekers, as guides, as examples, as companions. To be brothers and sisters in Christ.

Not only do they have these roles to play, but we need to let them know that our seekers need to be among them, participating in the active life of the church. Over the years, we've come to think of the catechumenate as something that happens outside of the community—in its own silo—until the catechumens are "ready" to join the rest of the parish family. Although we may be reticent to introduce the catechumens to the parish because every family has its flaws, we should welcome them into parish life right away.

Consider also that by not getting our seekers involved early and often in the life of the parish, we're denying them the opportunity to see Christ at work. For all the negative aspects of our communities, there are many more positive aspects that may not make as much noise but reveal Christ to us in the midst of our communities. Also, in my experience, it's our seekers who very often reveal Christ to the rest of our parishioners. It's a mutually beneficial relationship.

Catechizing Your Parish on Talking with Seekers

For those of you who are Star Trek fans, the term "first contact" has a special meaning—it's that moment when the Federation (typically humans) encounter an alien race for the first time. In the Star Trek universe, how well that first contact goes can have repercussions for generations, be it the positive relationship that developed with the Vulcans or the negative relationships that developed with the Romulans and the Klingons. Put another way, first impressions matter, and a bad first impression can be difficult to recover from.

These same first contact issues apply to our seekers. Since we all want to give a good first impression, we should help catechize our parishioners with some simple guidelines:

Be welcoming
Whenever talking with a seeker, be like Christ. It's an over-used phrase, but when approaching someone you don't know, ask yourself, "What would Jesus do?"

Know where information is available
Everyone in the parish should know who to contact when they encounter a seeker. This should be more than just directing them to the parish web site, bulletin, or parish office. Take an active role and exchange contact information with them so that you can then pass this on to your initiation team. Let the seeker know that you or someone else will get back with them very soon.

Be nonjudgmental
Everyone who meets a seeker needs to understand that this is the Holy Spirit at work. Regardless of the situation or circumstances, the Spirit has chosen this moment to bring this soul to us. And there is no right or wrong time for the Spirit to lead them to us. Our job is to hear them out and guide them to the right people as soon as possible. As I have often said, if the Holy Spirit is bringing them to my door right now, who am I to tell them to come back later?

Don't make any assumptions
This can be difficult, especially for initiation catechists, when meeting a seeker for the first time. During this first encounter, it is far too early to determine what the seekers' actual sacramental needs may be or what challenges they may face (particularly with marriage issues). The goal is to get them in

contact with the initiation team so they can start reviewing their situation in more detail.

Don't "register" them yet

Very often, the parish's first instinct is to get them registered for the parish and the initiation process. First contact, however, is not the time for paperwork. You certainly should exchange contact information (name, phone number, email address) so that you or someone on the initiation team can contact them, but it is better to avoid the term "registration." If the seeker brings it up, let them know that this will be done later. There's a certain formality and commitment when it comes to filling out forms and paperwork. We don't want them feeling like we've just sold them a used car. Most seekers are hesitant to "sign on the dotted line," and we need to respect that feeling.

Be alert to any preconceived notions they may have

Oftentimes, seekers have already done some research about becoming Catholic or the initiation process. Or they may have talked with friends who are Catholic or with others about the church. More often than not, much of this information is dated, misguided, or just flat-out wrong. First contact is not necessarily the time to start getting into the weeds about these particulars. If necessary, simply reassure the seekers that all may not be as they think and that everything will be made clear once they've talked with the initiation team.

What to say when asked "how long does it take?"

This is perhaps the number-one question seekers will ask, and our gut reaction is to give them a short direct answer. Don't do it! Steer away from any schedules or timelines. Instead, tell them that their journey through the initiation process is an individual one, and that one's time through the process depends on many different factors. You can assure them that once they've talked with an initiation team member, all these different factors will be reviewed in order to customize a process that will address their needs.

As Church, We're All Family

Seekers come to the church in a variety of ways, but more often than not, it starts with someone talking with a parishioner. Everyone in the parish—not just secretaries and ministers and catechists—needs to understand their duties when it comes to finding and working with our seekers.

Most importantly, we need to stop thinking of our seekers, catechumens, and candidates as people who are not members of the parish until they've completed their initiation. This is like thinking of your own child as not being a member of the family until they've graduated high school. As Catholics, we are all members of the Body of Christ, and we are all called to evangelize. So make sure everyone knows how to welcome a new seeker just like Christ.

Chapter 9

Come Join in the Dance
(Two Steps Forward, One Step Back)

As you begin moving to an ongoing year-round process, you will find that it's rarely straightforward. Even with the best planning, you may find yourself taking two steps forward and one step back as you move along. This is normal and nothing to be concerned about, as long as you keep making progress forward. Sometimes things don't work out as we expect; and sometimes things work better than expected. Even by following a good planning process (see chapter 7), there are always variables that can cause you to take a step back to evaluate.

The most important part of this dance is making sure you stay on the dance floor. When something doesn't go as planned or if the results are not quite what you expected, there can be a strong urge to just go back to what you were doing before. Resist that urge! There's a difference between taking a step back to evaluate and scrapping the whole thing. Remember why you started on this journey of change to begin with. Our older models of implementing the catechumenate can and must evolve with the needs of our seekers, our communities, and our church.

Where Do We Start?

Initiation catechists will often tell me that they want to move to an ongoing year-round process but they don't know where to start. It's a fair comment. And while I've already given a lot of advice in the earlier parts of this book, I realize that the reality of actually moving to a year-round process—or even making any changes to your existing process—can seem impossible. Don't worry. These feelings are normal. Let's walk through some suggestions of ways you can get started. I call this first step "finding the low-hanging fruit."

Find the Low-Hanging Fruit

Some of you may be familiar with the "low-hanging fruit" concept. Its origins come from business problem-solving techniques taught to managers as a way of approaching complex problems and improving efficiency. "Finding the low-hanging fruit" means identifying those problems that are small and easy to fix and addressing those before moving on to the bigger challenges. This accomplishes three things:

- It gets the group thinking about problems and how to solve them (which can be particularly difficult for those who have trouble seeing any problems).

- It identifies small problems that still need to be fixed, even if they don't play a big role in solving the larger problems.

- It provides the team with some quick, easy wins so they can build confidence in the process and move on to the bigger challenges.

It's as much a learning tool as it is a practical tool, because managers learn to identify problems as part of the process, which in turn helps them to unpack elements of larger issues. While this is a common business problem-solving strategy, it's also employed in the world of sports. For example, athletes identify those small things they can improve upon in an effort to boost their overall performance. It's a cumulative effect—lots of smaller wins make for a bigger win.

So I challenge you to look closely at your own initiation process and see if you can identify the low-hanging fruit. What are some of the smaller, easy-to-fix problems? Is the date and time of your catechetical sessions convenient for most of the seekers? Do your catechetical sessions conflict with other activities or group meetings at the parish? If that's the case, you might consider changing when you regularly meet or how often you hold sessions. Not only should you be asking yourself about these smaller issues, but I encourage you to have every member of your team do this. You might even want to ask some of your stakeholders to try this. Then schedule a meeting together to start to review these lists and prioritize them. The reason I suggest this as a group exercise is because it's always better to have more than one pair of eyes on the situation. Oftentimes, your team members may see something you don't or may have an innovative solution you didn't think of.

To help you identify some of your low-hanging fruit, here are a few questions you should ask of yourself and your process:

- What do your parish secretaries or staff do when someone asks about becoming Catholic?

- When people call and ask when your "classes" start, what do you say?

- When was the last time you sat down and talked with your seekers one on one?

- Does everyone in your process think of themselves as part of a group?

- Do other parishioners recognize or know the seekers in your process?

- When was the last time you sat down with your pastor to discuss the initiation process?

- Do you use academic terms to describe your initiation process?

- Does your parish have a school? How is it involved in the initiation process?

- Do you think your process is reaching all the different demographics within your parish?

- How do you handle the evangelization and precatechumenate phase?

- Have all the appropriate people on your team been through basic catechetical training?

- Has everyone on your team been through safe environment training?

- When was the last time you talked with a fellow initiation team member outside your parish?

- What's your process for adult Catholics seeking confirmation?

- How involved are you with planning the Easter Vigil?

- What happens in your parish over the summer?

- Do you make reading Scripture part of your catechetical sessions?

- Are all your seekers participating in Sunday Mass?

- What are the other local parishes doing for their initiation process?

- How many seekers do you carry over from one year to the next?

- Do you hold your catechetical sessions in a classroom?

- When was the last time you changed anything in how you facilitate your process?

- When was the last time you sat down with your team to evaluate your process?

- When was the last time you or any of your team went through catechumenate-specific training?

- When was the last time you went to your cathedral?

- How often do your participants engage in the discussions?

These questions are not in any particular order, nor are they all the questions you could ask. These are questions to get your juices flowing for finding the low-hanging fruit—something you can identify and fix easily that will get you one step closer to getting to your goal. And if you didn't notice, a number of these questions tie right back to everything else you've read in this book. Remember, you don't have to tackle all your problems at once, and you don't have to change everything overnight. Find and fix those few that are easy now, and give yourself time to strategize how to address other issues later. This is all part of your process-planning exercise.

Developing Short-Term Goals

Earlier in the book, I talked about the need to have a vision for your initiation process. That vision is your goal, and as I recommended, don't limit that vision. But getting there does take planning and time. Remember, in the initiation business we're playing the long game—conversion doesn't happen overnight. It's a steady process of building a relationship with Christ and his church. St. Peter's wasn't built in a day. Our processes aren't going to change overnight.

By finding the low-hanging fruit, however, you can identify those processes you can easily implement. The list of these items now become your short-term goals. For example, one short-term goal could be moving your evangelization and precatechumenate process from a group process to an individualized process:

Step one: Stop holding group sessions for the precatechumenate. Just take them off your calendar. Not only have you now freed up time on your calendar, you've freed up the people who do those group sessions—and their time.

Step two: Have those team members schedule informal one-on-one sessions with seekers. These are not teaching sessions. This is information gathering, both for you and the seeker. Nick Wagner's book *Seek the Living God: Five RCIA Inquiry Questions for Making Disciples* is an excellent guide on taking seekers through the evangelization and precatechumenate phase.

Step three: Recognize that there is no fixed time for evangelization and precatechumenate. We have a tendency to be obsessed with calendars and schedules and deadlines. The initiation process has no schedule. It has no deadlines. It takes what it takes, and how long that takes is determined by each individual seeker. In fact, this could be one short-term goal you can apply to the entire process. Let go of the calendar. When you do, you find there's a lot more room for the Holy Spirit to enter and take hold in your process.

The key to developing short-term goals is identifying those issues that are easier to fix, then developing the steps to fix them. Not sure what steps it will take to fix them? Seek help! This book is one tool to help you, but you should also reach out to others, both within and outside of your parish. TeamRCIA is one resource you can easily access for ideas and guidance in your ministry. We're all stronger when we work together.

Developing Long-Term Goals

If the low-hanging fruit become your short-term goals, what are your long-term goals? Remember that "vision" I asked you to think about? That is the basis for developing your long-term goals.

Let's assume your goal is to have a year-round process that develops true disciples. Sounds pretty lofty, right? But that's our vision. Our short-term goals are small steps to get us there. But how do we break down this vision into longer term goals? Let's start with the tools you need:

- Your team and key stakeholders

- To your right, the list of your low-hanging fruit—your short-term goals

- To your left, your vision, written down so you and everyone can see it

- In front of you, a five-year calendar and some paper and a pen

You will notice that we need your team and key stakeholders as part of this exercise. To be most effective, this needs to be a group exercise. Why? Because if any plan is going to work, it needs consensus and buy-in from all your team and stakeholders. Without their buy-in and cooperation, it will be particularly difficult. Remember, it's the parish that's responsible for the initiation of seekers, and if certain members can't get on board with the plan, it can cause misunderstandings and derision. We want to avoid that.

Because we want all these people to participate, we must schedule this meeting so that everyone can attend. That's no small task for many parishes. But this doesn't need to be a long, drawn-out process. I've seen parishes make this kind of exercise a full-day retreat. I've seen others make this a one- or two-hour meeting. This is fully dependent on your parish and how your team thinks it can best be accomplished. Personally, I'm all for day-long retreats, but the reality of booking all these people into one full day is particularly challenging, especially for pastors. So talk with your pastor up front and see what's possible. Maybe an all-day retreat works for everyone else, but you can only have your pastor for an hour or two. That's fine. Work around that. The key is having him on board with the plan.

Neither does this gathering need to be as involved as a one-day retreat. I've seen parishes make this an easy two-hour meeting with a few breaks. The bottom line is that you need to consider what works best for your parish. I know some communities that are happy to have this be a long exercise. Most communities I've encountered, however, don't often have the time to gather too many people together like this for an extended period. Do what's best for your parish. But the basic format is going to look something like this:

Step one: Start breaking your vision into identifiable goals. For example, if the vision is to have a year-round process, one goal is to develop a year-round calendar. And what might that one-year calendar look like? Look at your typical parish calendar for a start and see how the initiation process can be integrated into all the activities of the parish. If your vision is to create true disciples through your process, how might that be accomplished? This might mean talking with those who have gone through the process and getting their feedback—finding out what worked and didn't work for them. As you identify these goals, write them down.

Step two: Pull out your calendars and see when you can start accomplishing these goals. How might your short-term goals help you accomplish these longer-term goals? Now look at your five-year calendar. Will it actually take five years to get to your vision? Not necessarily. I suggest a five-year calendar to give yourself permission to stretch out your implementation. This is the same permission we need to allow ourselves to let our seekers take as long as necessary to get through the initiation process. When you consider that the National Statutes for the Catechumenate says that the period of the catechumenate "should extend for at least one year in formation" (6) after the Rite of Acceptance, in order to accommodate a full liturgical year of Sunday Masses, then many of our seekers will continue on from one year to the next.

The five-year calendar also reminds you that you don't want to drag out the process. Mind you, if you follow the project-planning cycle in chapter 7, you will never truly be finished with your implementation. As you evaluate your process every year, you will always find new ways to improve your process. It's an ever-evolving thing that will never be complete or finished but always changes to adapt to the needs of the community. But neither do you want to keep kicking the can down the path as a way of avoiding real and substantive change to your process.

Step three: Now that you have your short-term and long-term goals, your calendar roughed out with timetables for implementation, and your vision statement, go once more around the room to make sure there is consensus. If you have anyone who disagrees with the plan, it may require some "off-line" discussion with that person. Recognize their concerns, and schedule some time to go over their concerns one on one. A word of warning: Be prepared for the fact that not everyone may get on board with your new plan. Old ways die hard, and not everyone handles change easily, particularly if they don't think change is necessary. On the other hand, if you can convince them to give it a try, and they can begin to see fruit from the endeavor, you just might bring them on board. But always be prepared for the fact that you may lose some team members.

Maintaining Focus

One of our biggest issues is that we're so focused on what's in front of us, we tend to lose sight of the bigger picture. This is especially true during Lent, when we're leading some of our catechumens on those final steps toward initiation. We get so busy with the day-to-day and the week-to-week that we find ourselves caught in the moment. We get so focused on just getting them in, getting them out, and getting things done that we can lose perspective—lose focus—of our long-term vision. We tell ourselves that we'll take time to look at this later, but too often, we never do.

The other problem (though to a much lesser extent) is that we spend so much time on the long-term vision of our initiation process that we fail to notice what needs attention right in front of us. Not only are the catechumens and candidates unsure of what to expect or what's going on, but our team members also get lost. We end up missing a lot of details as we look on down the road without noticing the potholes right in front of us.

So how do we make sure we're focusing on the right things? We need to follow some of our own advice: We need to make the time periodically. Make time to meet with your team. Find and attend training workshops or retreats. Find resources online. It's never too early to start thinking about these sorts of activities for you and your team, so make them part of your schedule and commit to them.

Lastly, take time to pray and invite the Holy Spirit into your efforts.

Chapter 10

Detour Ahead:
Some Odds and Ends

I've done my best to lay out a road map for moving to an ongoing year-round process that should lead to success in your parish. But as with any journey, you will likely face some obstacles. The path you take may not be the same as I outline here nor be the same as what has worked in other parishes. My goal is to provide some of the basic concepts that will lead you in the right direction, along with some practical advice that worked for my parish. But always remember, church is a team effort. We do our best when we can lean on one another—those within our parishes and those outside of our parishes who have the knowledge and experience from having traveled these roads before.

While it is impossible to address every issue we may face in this ministry, I do want to mention a few that I've had to address on a regular basis.

Turning Inquiry Calls into Catechetical Moments

I field a lot of telephone calls, emails, and text messages regularly from seekers. And these could come from a variety of people.

Some are Catholics looking for confirmation, and some are looking for (what they think is) the RCIA. The most common question?—When do your classes start? But if you made it all the way through to this last chapter of the book, you've already read my advice and comments on that particular question.

What I want to emphasize here is the need to engage these callers—these would-be seekers—in conversation. Far too often, these calls are viewed as simply informational. Instead, we need to look at all these calls as an opportunity for evangelization and catechesis.

What these callers might think is a simple question is almost always not the case. Context is everything, so make the effort to dig deeper and find out why they're calling. Sometimes they are just "shopping around." Sometimes they're calling because they think they need to be confirmed or go through adult baptism classes in order to be married in the church (which is a common misconception). Oftentimes, they're calling based on obsolete or inadequate information. All of these moments are opportunities.

At the very least, these calls are an opportunity for some much-needed catechesis. At worst, you spend some extra time on a call, but at best, there's a chance to bring these people closer to Christ and his church.

Find Ways to Say Yes or to Break through the Bureaucracy

I took a phone call recently from someone we'll call Raul. Raul was an active, catechized Catholic, but he had never been confirmed. He was looking to celebrate confirmation so that he could be a godparent to his nephew, a noble gesture indeed! Raul was not a member of our parish and had been calling around to all the local parishes because he kept running into roadblocks. One parish told him he needed to go through the catechumenate, which, for them, didn't start until September. Not only was this start date long after his nephew's scheduled baptism, but as a catechized baptized Catholic, he didn't belong in the catechumenate process.

Still other parishes said they didn't have a separate adult confirmation preparation process or that their process didn't start until several months later.

The more I talked with Raul, the more I got to know about him and his situation—something it seemed none of these other parishes took the effort to do. Because of that, my goal was to make the extra effort to help Raul get confirmed in time for his nephew's baptism. I didn't want to be the next person to say no to him. After some more discussion and consideration, we were able to find a way to help. In Raul's case, we learned that one of our regional bishops was celebrating a rite of confirmation before his nephew's baptism. Another possibility was that Raul's pastor could ask the bishop for a special dispensation so that Raul could serve as his nephew's godparent.

My point is that, too often, we get locked into our established processes and end up turning away people like Raul rather than trying to find ways to minister to them.

Now ask yourself, what would Jesus do in this situation? My dear brothers and sisters, sometimes we are our own worst enemies when seekers come to our door. It's easier for us to blame the problem on the caller for their not knowing proper procedures or to blame the seemingly impossible bureaucracy of the church as we turn these people away. But very often, we haven't made a good effort to dig deeper and try to help them. In case you haven't noticed, it's gotten far less difficult to find an open seat for Mass. We can't afford to turn people away. I guarantee you, Raul is going to remember how we went out of our way to help, and that act of kindness is going to be reflected in his own openness to Christ. As a church, we are far too quick to say no. We need to find ways to say yes.

Addressing Marriage and Annulment Issues

One of our biggest issues is having to address marriage situations with our seekers. Given that they come from a variety of backgrounds, it is inevitable. If you haven't had to address them already, you will likely have to address them in the future. Since we tend to be on the front lines as these issues arise, we should be better prepared. So here are some tips on addressing marriage and annulment issues:

- **Educate yourself about marital issues and the annulment process.** Spend some time with your pastor or his designated minister to learn more about the annulment process and what's involved. Look to see if your diocese or local tribunal offers some kind of training. The more you know about the process, the more comfortable you will be when talking with seekers about these issues. Most importantly, make sure you discuss with your pastor what the procedures should be when you have someone who needs to have any marriage issues addressed.

- **Do try to find out as soon as possible.** We should be learning about any marriage issues during the period of evangelization and precatechumenate. The sooner we learn of any issues, the more time we have to get them resolved. This can be a problem because some seekers are hesitant to reveal these details. Make sure they understand that this is a safe space.

- **Don't make any promises.** Even if you have some knowledge and experience with marriage issues, your place is not to make any judgments or decisions. Our job is to be welcoming, compassionate listeners as we direct them to those who can best help them. Also, try to allay their fears. There is a lot of misinformation about the annulment process, so we need to be supportive and remain positive.

- **Do allow them to participate in the process.** Seekers should never be turned away. They should be welcomed into the formation process. They should go through the Rite of Acceptance (or Rite of Welcoming), provided all other conditions of preparation for those rites are evident (though you should check with your diocesan bishop's office to be sure there are no local restrictions on this). They should participate in Mass and participate in the active life of the parish. This can actually help them cope better as they go through the annulment process.

- **Don't have them go through the Lenten rites until any marriage issues have been resolved.** For catechumens, the Rite of Election is strictly reserved for those who have no sacramental impediments. Similarly, those candidates who are already baptized need to have any marriage issues resolved before they can be received into full communion in the Catholic Church. Ideally, all these conditions should be fully disclosed during the period of evangelization and precatechumenate so there are no surprises, expectations, or delays.

Working with Those Who Have Special Needs

This may be an uncomfortable issue for many of us if we've never had any experience working with people who have special needs. First and foremost, we need to remember that Christ is open to everyone! If you don't have any experience working with special needs, seek help. That help may be in your own parish, or it may be available from your diocese or from another local parish. Find out who in your parish has experience with people who have special needs and see if they're willing to be a sponsor. The key is to be flexible. Learn your seeker's capabilities and make adjustments as needed. For more guidance, refer to the *Guidelines for the Celebration of the Sacraments with Persons with Disabilities*, available from the United States Conference of Catholic Bishops.

The Importance of Validating a Seeker's Baptism

Many of our seekers come to us having already been baptized as infants. That baptism could have been done through a Catholic parish, or it could have been done in another Christian tradition. Regardless of where or when it was done, we need to do our due diligence to determine the validity of that baptism because a person's baptismal status has bearing on the ritual path they need to follow.

It is also important to understand that this may not always be as simple as you might think. Baptized as an infant, they have no memory of the moment, so they're dependent on what their parents or godparents or other family members may have told them, and sometimes these sources are not always available or reliable. And they may or may not have any documentation of the event (certificate, photographs, for example).

Typically, if they were baptized in a Catholic parish in the United States and no longer have their baptismal certificate, it's fairly easy to validate their baptism. What is necessary is the name and location of the parish and the approximate date. If they were baptized outside of the United States, it can be much more challenging. In cases where it is impossible to track down parish records, we must rely on eyewitness testimony or photographs.

If they were baptized in another Christian tradition, we need to determine if that church's baptism is considered valid. If you or your pastor are not sure, your diocese can assist because they generally maintain a list of denominations whose baptisms are considered valid. The majority of mainline Christian churches follow a valid Trinitarian formula, but not all. And not all Christian churches issue certificates or maintain records as well as most Catholic churches. Here again, eyewitness testimony or photographs can serve as evidence.

If we "confess one baptism" as we say in our Nicene Creed, we owe it to our seekers to make the extra effort that may sometimes be needed. Most importantly, we need to validate their baptism so we can help these seekers see the validity and dignity of their own baptism. I've had a number of seekers feel as though their baptism wasn't valid as a result of our lack of effort. Still others didn't understand why we couldn't just baptize them again. For their sake and ours, we need to do our due diligence.

Baptized Catholics

As with all seekers who were baptized as infants, determining the path a baptized Catholic needs to take is dependent on whether they've been catechized. It's not unusual for someone to have been baptized as an infant but never receive any formation in the faith or receive any other sacraments. These seekers fit the definition established in the United States National Statutes for the Catechumenate, which says:

> Although baptized adult Catholics who have never received catechetical instruction or been admitted to the sacraments of confirmation and Eucharist are not catechumens, some elements of the usual catechumenal formation are appropriate to their preparation for the sacraments, in accord with the norms of the ritual. ("Preparation of Uncatechized Adults for Confirmation and Eucharist," 25)

In other words, while they do not follow the same ritual path as those who are seeking baptism, they do follow a similar catechetical path. As with all our seekers, that catechetical path doesn't have a predetermined time frame, but it should be consistent with those established for catechumens (National Statutes 6 and RCIA 75). How long that journey may be is determined during their journey through the period of evangelization and precatechumenate.

I have also had some seekers who were baptized Catholic as infants but do not fit the definition of "uncatechized." Some of these people were essentially raised in the faith, attending Mass regularly with their families, but they never received confirmation or Eucharist. That's not to say that they don't need any additional preparation, but neither does it mean they have to follow a similar catechetical path as those who are completely uncatechized. Here again, how much preparation they need is determined during their journey through the period of evangelization and precatechumenate. And since these Catholics are catechized, they do not participate in any of the rites for those who are uncatechized (see RCIA 400). In my parish, these catechized Catholics celebrate their confirmation (and, if needed, Eucharist) when the bishop comes for the parish celebration of confirmation. Of course, your diocese may have different protocols, so always check with your local bishop's office.

Catechized Christians

Some of our seekers come to us having been baptized and having some formation in non-Catholic Christian faiths. Some may have been active in their churches. Now they are coming to our door wanting to become Catholic or, more appropriately, wanting to come into full communion with the Catholic Church.

It would not be appropriate to treat someone with this background the same as those who are uncatechized. I mention this because I have had some experiences with people who felt that just because someone was not catechized in the Catholic tradition, they should be considered uncatechized and have to follow a catechetical path similar to the uncatechized. That is not the case. The rite states:

> Anything that would equate candidates for reception with those who are catechumens is to be absolutely avoided. (477)

As with all our seekers, we should take them through the process of evangelization and precatechumenate. This, as with all our other seekers, allows us to get to know their stories while they begin to learn our story. This will help us determine how much additional formation they may need. Refer to RCIA 473–486 for more details on guiding these candidates.

Children

So far I have not mentioned anything with regard to children and the catechumenate. That was intentional. Everything I've written here is with consideration to an adult audience in mind (see chapter 4, Treating Adults as Adults). Working with children is an entirely different dynamic and would necessitate an entirely separate book. (For more on this, see *Children and Youth in the Catechumenate: Forming Young Disciples for Mission* by Anne Y. Koester [Liturgical Press].)

For the moment, I will refer you to RCIA 252–259. These paragraphs go into detail with regard to the "Christian Initiation of Children Who Have Reached Catechetical Age."

But on the topic of children as it relates to adults in the RCIA, I will leave you with these thoughts: Do everything you can to help those adults with childcare issues participate in your adult formation and initiation processes. There's no reason why an infant can't be brought in with their parents to a session (I used to do this with my own children). I've also seen parishes set up childcare with teen volunteers during their sessions. Again, in my own parish, we've had older children do homework in an adjacent room during our sessions. There's no reason why a seeker who is a parent (particularly a single parent) should feel that they can't go through or continue with the process due to a lack of childcare. Here again, the Holy Spirit has called them to us now. So we should do our best to make arrangements to include them, whether it's providing childcare or offering alternatives to catechetical sessions. Remember, our catechetical sessions are not the primary means of catechesis—they are only a secondary support tool. Sunday Mass and active participation in the community are the primary forms of catechesis. Missing Sunday Mass is a far more serious issue than missing a catechetical session.

Conclusion

As a traveler who's been on the road for some time, I appreciate what I've learned from those who have traveled with me and before me. I also recognize my obligation to share that experience and knowledge with those around me and coming up behind me. 1 Peter reminds us:

> As each one has received a gift, use it to serve one another as good stewards of God's varied grace. (1 Pet 4:10)

We are all but stewards of the faith while we are here, so I hope my experiences can help you navigate a route to a process that is ongoing, year-round, and apprentice-driven. My hope is that this will lead to developing true disciples for Christ and his church, so that they too can be good stewards and pass it on.